Watch Out!

We are MBA

Attention Authors

Manas Publications is waging a war to tell the world that India can win battles, not only by bullet, but also by pen. We are converting fighters into writers since there is no dearth of intellectuals in our country but their knowledge is confined to them only. No sincere effort has been made by any other publisher to give the right direction to their knowledge and the talent of an intellectual remains hidden. An author always gives the raw material in the shape of manuscript and it is the sense of a publisher to make it a finished product. We have been motivating the intellectual mind and publishing their manuscripts for more than two decades and we would like to publish your manuscript too. If you or your colleagues have any manuscript or are working on it, please don't hesitate to contact us, with detailed synopsis and contents, for its publication. We take utmost care in production and give a wide publicity to the book and its author. We can also suggest you the title for the writing related to your subject, as we are the publishers who believe more in quality than in quantity.

Watch Out!

We are MBA

A Nobel by

Nishant Kaushik

Manas Publications
New Delhi-110002 (INDIA)

MANAS PUBLICATIONS
(Publishers, Distributors, Importers & Exporters)
4402/5A, Main Ansari Road
(Adjacent to Bank of Baroda)
Darya Ganj, New Delhi-110 002 (INDIA)
Off. © 23260783, 23265523, Res. © 23842660
Fax: 011-23272766
E-mail: manaspublications@vsnl.com
www.manaspublications.in

ISBN 978-81-7049-322-8
Rs. 495/-

Typeset at
Manas Publications

Printed in India at
R.K. Offset, Delhi
and Published by Mrs Suman Lata for
Manas Publications, 4402/5A, Main Ansari Road
(Adjacent Bank of Baroda)
Darya Ganj, New Delhi-110 002 (INDIA)

FOR

My late grandfather, who first encouraged me with the art of story-telling as he tirelessly listened to and lovingly admired all the fairy tales I narrated to him as a toddler

TO

The MBA batch of 2006, NMIMS, Mumbai—for providing me with two of the most glorious years of my life

Preface

"Chuck the mushy statements, please! I am going to keep a track of how many of you actually keep in touch with me five years from now!"

"Save yourself the trouble—I am telling you right now, I won't!"

A moment of light banter observed on one of the last days on campus, April 2006.

The characters depicted in the book are fictional, yet not entirely so. And while this story is set in a B-school environment, its essence is not limited to a B-school. The protagonist, Nakul Kapoor, is a reflection of all friends, colleagues and acquaintances I have come across and known during school, undergrad and post-grad college life alike. He is an entity that amalgamates the thousand emotions we experience at our age. Like each one of us, he harbours certain aspirations—to love, to be loved, and to be successful.

The story is an account of Nakul's journey of two years in a premier MBA institute in Mumbai with his friends, with whom he shares his dreams, desires, and peeves. En route, emotions are born, nurtured, and in some ways, injured too. Eventually, Nakul reaches a point of reconciliation to the fact that not all dreams transcend Utopian boundaries to get fulfilled in actuality.

Nishant Kaushik

Acknowledgements

When I first conceived the idea of writing a book on our experiences at B-school, I had mentioned it in mere passing, almost in jest, to my friend Parikshit (PJ), while we sat in a coffee shop vegetating idly after our placements. From that day till now, there have been numerous contributions from various people that have helped me on this journey.

My parents and close family members: for the love and support I have got from them in all my endeavours. I love you all.

Kamini, PJ and Abhijit: my mentors and friends throughout, who offered their invaluable inputs in enhancing the content of my work. I also thank Google Talk, without which we could not have stayed wired, given the huge distances!

Abhay, Swarnim, Saurabh, Avik, Nidhi and Varuna: A few of my close friends, and some of the most instrumental factors in motivating me to write this book.

The 6MM folk: My roomies in Mumbai, with whom I spent some unforgettable glorious days of my life.

Over the year that I spent writing this book, several people helped me in various ways from offering their suggestions to giving a simple word of encouragement. Just some of the names that must get special mention are my friends Ashish, Kshitij, Purujeet, Vaibhav, Nimish, Sarang, Kinchit, Gaurav (GP), Gaurav (GJ), Rashmi, Dinesh, Hanoz, KK, Kulin, Ekta, Aamna, Santanu, Aanandita, Aditi and Abhishek.

A special note of thanks to Mr. Ajay Tomar for his tireless support to my effort.

Last but not the least, I thank my editor and the entire team of Manas Publications, for showing faith in my work and helping it see the light of the day.

Contents

CHAPTER 1

I Have Come Here Only to Have Fun

June 14, 2004. 8:40 A.M. I came out hurriedly from the shower, put on my best clothes, and went about rummaging the room to find all the requisite documents. I read my offer letter from the institute once again.

Kindly ensure you carry with you the following:

- ❑ ***Your offer letter***
- ❑ ***Your fee receipt***
- ❑ ***Certificates of marks for class 10 and 12***
- ❑ ***Your migration certificate from graduation college***

'P.S.: Kindly ensure that you reach the college at 9 A.M sharp. We deem punctuality and discipline to be of utmost importance, and they form an integral part of our value system.'

Blast! I am never going to be able to make it by 9... The postscript already had my head spinning as it portended the critical need of bringing about a few radical changes in my nature. Something told me I was going to face a nice grind at this new place, and I was going to have to give up the luxury of a half-hour bath I was so used to back home, if I were to fulfill their "punctuality" criterion. Discipline had a different definition in everyone's context anyway, so I decided not to fret too much about it.

'Are you ready Nakul? You are getting late, you know', my mother said.

'Yes ma, I know, but I can't seem to find my fee receipt. Can you please help me?'

'For God's sake, now, Nakul! You are going to be an MBA soon- you are no longer a primary school kid.'

'Please ma, we really don't have time for this discussion now', I said, as I saw my fee receipt crumpled inside my wallet. I thanked my stars and stuffed it into my pocket before my mother noticed it, else I would have had to face a barrage of words reminding me about how innately careless and clumsy I had always been.

I quickly stuffed all the documents in a folder and plunked myself on the backseat of the car with my parents. With ten minutes to go before it struck nine, I was now quite certain that I was going to rub the authorities the wrong side by breaking an important norm of their value system. *How many more elements must be there in this value system that I would have to adhere to? Were they going to hand me a pink slip for coming late, like those scores of pink slips I got in my school life?* A myriad of anxious thoughts clouded my mind even as our car made its way through the bustling roads of Mumbai.

'It looks rather squat,' I commented on the picture of the campus building as I scanned the college brochure, 'hardly what a post-graduate campus should look like.'

'You can't expect better in Mumbai.' My mother reasoned. 'Everything is so packed here there is hardly any land.'

I couldn't agree more. I peeped out of my car window and observed hordes of multi-storeyed apartments and commercial complexes glued together, and whatever space that yielded, gave way to wafer-thin lanes and by-lanes, each clogged with more vehicles than it could afford. Yet, there was an alluring aura about the city that everyone spoke of. I had not been able to recognize it then, but once I would, it was to bound me with permanence to the city.

'The size of the campus is anyway hardly important,' my father said. 'What you must know is that you have made it to one of the best B-schools and we are proud of you. But you must recognize that this is but a mere opening you've got. The onus is now on you to get the best out of it.'

'I agree,' I nodded, 'but there should at least be a hostel on campus. The boys' hostel here is out of campus premises, about a kilometer away. And worse, the girls' hostel is in the opposite direction, another mile or so away.'

'I hope you are not too upset about that, Nakul?' Dad snapped. 'You know what you are here for, right? Let other necessities of life take their own course of time, please.'

'I didn't mean that, I just said it in passing...'

'Yeah, but it conveyed what it had to.'

'No, I just...' My voice trailed off. There was no sense arguing on that point. Much that I would try, I could not mask the dismay I had felt on learning about the hostel arrangements, especially the distance that separated the two hostels. My parents would view my dismay differently, but the disappointment was simply because the arrangement did not give the feel that a typical residential program should give.

'Look here, there are a few things I've kept for you in this bag', my father continued. 'This diary has a list of all contacts I have in Mumbai, just in case there is an emergency you can get in touch with any of them. I have bought this new raincoat that you are going to need very soon. And please get rid of that lousy windcheater of yours. It won't help in these torrential rains, and moreover it's a very obscene colour.'

My mother chipped in: 'And please get a haircut now. Your long sideburns look atrocious.' My mother had a major aversion towards my hair. I often dreamt I was Samson, and my mother had summoned someone to chop off my tresses while I was asleep. 'You should feel relieved now, though,' she continued. 'I won't be around now to pester you to use a comb to brush your hair!' She immediately looked out of the window, and I knew she was in tears. But I decided to fake ignorance, as it would not help anyway to try and comfort her. I had always been the apple of her eye, the typical, pampered, younger child. It would take them a while to get used to my not being at home, but they would, after a while.

After a 25-minute frenzied drive through the traffic clutter, we reached the institute. My watch showed 9:20 AM. *So much for punctuality.*

'Do you want us to come in?' Dad asked as I got down.

'No, don't worry, I'll handle it.' I stopped them. 'The formalities could take long- issuing the identity card, the briefing session, etc. I don't want you to unnecessarily wait for hours in the corridor.'

As I saw them leave, I stood still for a moment, and recalled the affection and tireless support I always received from them. And probably for the first time, I realized how lucky and blessed I was to have parents like them.

Looking at the building from closer quarters, it looked even more cramped. The front entrance had a small porch that could accommodate no more than one car at a time. The main lobby overlooked a small lawn, each square foot of which was occupied by students from the senior batch, sipping on *cutting chai* and engaging in idle chitchat in the recess. There was no sprawling landscaping, no modish state-of-the-art architectural effect of the campus. Yet the simple arrangement had a queer charm, largely on account of the cleanliness that it could boast of. Each corner of the building had a spic-n-span look, which was indicative of the effort the housekeeping might be putting in every day. The rear end of the lobby, near the dean's office, had a waiting room for visitors, bedecked with elegant furnishings. Behind the lawn, on either side of the canteen, stood a line of small kiosks, serving an assorted variety of mid-meal snacks and juices, ranging from *dosas* to burgers and *vada pav*, providing a dainty setting to the ambience.

I entered the marble-floored corridor and sought directions. A large digital screen displayed:

MBA BATCH OF 2004-'06: CLASSROOM # 28

I shot up four flights of stairs, my heart racing, and hoping that I would be spared a rebuke in public for having violated the punctuality criterion. I opened the door meekly, and saw a rotund figure near the blackboard. If I remember well, he was speaking something on group dynamics and interpersonal skills, when I interrupted him. 'Excuse me Sir, may I…?'

'This lecture or the next?' The professor growled, strands from his extra furry moustache trembling under the jet of air his huge nostrils let out. Through the spectacles perched on his nose, two eyes looked at me with a tinge of loathe.

'This…' I mumbled.

'Then what are you waiting for sonny? You are more than half an hour late already. Please come in and take your seat!'

I got a queasy feeling when I saw around one hundred and twenty eyes turn towards me in unison as I scampered to the corner seat in the last row. I tried hard to concentrate on the interpersonal skills *pravachan* (campus lingo for a hackneyed lecture) the professor was delivering, but was too busy looking around the class, making note of each student. *Blow!! Forty-eight boys versus twelve girls! Something's grossly wrong here,* I said to myself in dismay.

I finally turned to see the girl seated beside me, but consciously abstained from staring too long, lest she may take me for a lecherous creep and spread the news to the other damsels as well. She had put some enormous quantity of a nauseating perfume- jasmine, maybe. I concluded her father must own some factory of perfumes back home. I didn't care much, and if I were to have it my way, I would have loved to put on my nose one of those clips put on the clothes hanging on our clothesline in the backyard.

'Alright, now that I've introduced myself and spoken quite a bit myself,' said the professor, 'why doesn't each one of you give an introduction to the class too? Let's start with you, young lady!' He pointed to a girl sitting in the front row.

'Good morning class! My name is Simran Dutta; I come from Delhi, and have done my bachelors in telecom engineering.'

'Hi! I am Viral Patel from Ahmedabad, B.E Chemical Engineering. I've worked in a private firm for a year and a half.'

'Arun Jain, Pune, B.Com, two years work experience with Madison Media.'....

'Hi, I am Nakul Kapoor from Chandigarh. I have completed my bachelors in Instrumentation Engineering, and have no work experience whatsoever.' I made note of the fact that I lay special emphasis on the word "completed". I felt a sense of immense pride and satisfaction to find that I had passed those four years of drudgery, filled with horrifying subjects, without too many hiccups.

'Hi, my name is Abhinav Chaudhary. I have come here only to have fun. I suggest we begin a club in our batch, give it a jazzy name-say for example, "The Fun Cell". Cool no? We'll initiate various activities under the aegis of this cell, through which we can have a lot of...er...fun! You know, games and picnics and all!'

I sat with my mouth agape even as the class burst into peals of laughter. I was grateful he mentioned "games and picnics" at the end of his statement, else I was going to let my imagination run wild.

Hundred introductions later, I had garnered a fair idea of the eclectic mix of the class I sat in. Amidst those descriptions of diverse backgrounds echoed one common aspiration that had sought this place as the medium to achieve it. In the adjoining class sat another division of the batch of equal strength, and presumably a similar mix. (For sake of convenience, the mammoth batch of 120 had been divided into two different classes.) And in the large crowd, I stood with an aspiration of my own, though it was just a bit too nebulous then.

The introductory pleasantries lasted till lunch. As I began to make my way down to the canteen, a voice called out from behind.

'Excuse me, first year is it?'

I turned back to see in front of me a sprightly guy, sporting a chic Ralph Lauren tee, funky linen trousers and a wide, sunshine smile. There are some people you can instantly relate to. Aryan Nair was just not one of them. The vivacity in his smile, combined with a conspicuously suave metropolitan accent, set him considerably apart from a relatively sedate, run-of-the-mill Nakul. I could not have imagined then, that we would discover among ourselves a bunch of common likes, peeves, apprehensions and dreams that would unite us in a friendship that would stand the test of time.

'Yes, Nakul is the name. What about you?' I stretched my hand.

'I'm Aryan. I've just come from Delhi. I guess I've missed the first class, right?'

'Yeah, nothing much happened though. The expected intro and all. So how come you're so late? You couldn't find the place?'

'No *yaar*, my flight was late by almost two hours. I'm coming straight from the airport. Look!'

He was loaded with a jumbo suitcase and a heavily stuffed air bag. 'It looks so....silly!'

'Don't bother,' I said, 'keep this aside for now. Let's go down, I'm really hungry.'

'Sure, but can you tell me where do I put this bag for now? I am feeling kind of weird. I haven't even seen my hostel room as yet!'

'Relax, don't fret! I saw mine yesterday, and I guess the condition of all rooms is alike. We can sure live with it for two years!'

As we strolled around the campus during the break, I saw a few guys already beginning to get fresh with the chicks. A lot of them probably found the four-to-one sex ratio pretty intimidating, and they realized something needed to be done fast. It is common belief, and fairly true too, that a select chunk of boys of any given batch, who are among the more proactive ones, have it in them to attract the pool of all the interesting girls. The laggards, the plain reactive ones, would normally lose out to this first mover advantage. Admittedly, I found myself in the latter half category, not so much for the lack of courage as much for the lack of someone interesting enough to pursue. For a long time to come, I was to find pleasure and amusement in simply watching other guys explore their chances. One of them was wandering about alone, as though looking out for a handkerchief to fall the *filmy* way, so he could pick it up, return it to the owner, and get a chance to introduce himself to someone. I had seen the likes of Rajendra Kumar and Kamal Hassan do it with perfect ease in the movies, but this guy was probably getting a bit too hopeful.

We were just about to enter the canteen, when Jasmine Perfume intercepted us. Thankfully, we were standing close to the kitchen, and the obnoxious smell of her perfume was being superimposed by the aroma of *missal pav* and *vada sambhar.*

'Hi, so how did you like the class? We didn't speak in the class in spite of sitting right next to each other. Ain't that strange?'

Not quite!

'Yeah indeed it is. I am Nakul, and this is Aryan.'

'Nice meeting you. I'm Sneha.'

'Good to meet you Sneha.' Aryan said. 'Nice perfume, by the way!'

Sorry?

'Thanks!' she beamed. 'It's jasmine. Original!'

'Wow, that's the best!' Aryan chuckled. 'Anyway, we got to go. See you around.'

'Bye. Bye, Nakul! Catch you later.'

No, please don't! 'So long, then.'

'Do you mind if I asked you a question?' I asked Aryan as we took our seats right in the middle of the cafeteria. 'Did you really think the smell of that perfume was so worth raving about?'

'Are you kidding dude?' Aryan sniggered. 'If I were her, I'd use it as a substitute for DDT!'

'Yeah, well…so?'

'It's just that she's a girl Nakul! You don't mess with them as long as they don't trouble you. So I always steer clear. Try and rub them the wrong way and they will snap back at you harder.'

'Point noted, boss!'

I ordered a plate of *samosas* and iced tea, and Aryan called for a whole wheat sandwich.

'Too much oil in the *samosas*,' he said. 'It's fattening. It nullifies all that I work out at the gym.' I took a deep breath and sucked my tummy in, and fluffed my shirt out a little. I stretched my neck as high as possible to hide my double chin. I looked at Aryan's well-drawn jaw-line, V-shaped body structure, and realized that my body looked no more than a globe-shaped head placed on a 6-foot 2-inch stocky frame of mass.

As we sat busily gobbling up the food, I looked around to peruse my surroundings and try and assess all the new faces around me. The table adjacent to ours had a group of four guys who looked no less than three years older than me, and were discussing the merits of their prior work experience. Behind us there was some Mr. Wise Guy who had caught some fake American accent, apparently as fast as an infant would catch a cold on being exposed to a dry winter breeze. With him were two girls, none of who showed an iota of interest in his stories about the adventure trips he had been to before coming to Mumbai. Then there were two pseudo chicks sitting at the far end of the café, and though I couldn't hear them, their animated discussion suggested that they were either discussing their respective boyfriends back home, or had found the first three hours of college sufficient to find a third girl worth bitching about.

Just then, a cheerful loud voice diverted my attention.

'Hey guys, mind if we share the table with you? This café is pretty small for a batch of our size, I must say!'

We looked up to see two guys standing at our table. One looked like a reincarnation of some rock star, bouncing a little up and down as he spoke. Every few seconds, he would crane his neck to check if a hottie was around, and if there would be one, the bounce would get just a little more bouncy. The other was a total contrast. Relatively demure, yet with a stroke of confidence in his persona, he looked like the son of the typical family drama movies of the 80s, an epitome of honesty, sincerity and commitment.

'Sure, pull two chairs.' said Aryan. 'By the way, I am Aryan.'

'I am Sameer Basu,' said the rock star reincarnate. 'But you can call me S.B. I have come from Calcutta. This is my e-friend, Swapnil Saxena from Gwalior. We communicated earlier online while preparing for our MBA entrance.'

'Hi, how do you do?' Swapnil shook hands with us. His voice was plainly unsophisticated, and had a touch of genuineness in it. He was clearly a person who was not conscious of his appearance, which was apparent from the random growth of stubble on his rather skinny face, and unkempt hair falling on his temples like that of a German Poodle. Yet he carried with him a charisma that would make every eligible girl's parents want her to marry him. He carried a look of maturity which parents like mine would want to cite as an example for their wayward children to learn a lesson or two.

After waiting for a while, Sameer continued, 'By the way, do any of you know what S.B stands for?'

'Yes, Sex Bomb, I think!' I said. 'But then why should we call you so?' I laughed.

'Hey, I am not that bad, am I?' S.B protested.

'Na, not at all! You are pretty good, in fact!' replied Aryan. 'You've got a marked style.'

Sameer nodded his head in acknowledgement like Aryan had just made a very matter-of-fact statement. Aryan resumed eating his whole wheat sandwich, carefully chewing each small molecule, lest any undigested particles may get deposited as lumps of unwanted fat on him. Swapnil had his eyes closed and was muttering a prayer, with his plate of *chana bhatura* lying in front of him. *Always pray before you eat. Thank the Almighty for giving you your daily bread,* I remembered Fr. Alberts tell us in class 4. Sameer sat with his neck stooped low, apparently trying to check out the tanned legs of a short skirted chick on the next table. I sat quietly in deep thought. *What's in store for me here? Will I cope with the expectations this course has from me? Will I make the right friends? Will I follow anything in any of the finance lectures? .... Will I get a good job?*

CHAPTER 2

The Wooer and The Wooed

Meanwhile, in another corner of the campus, stood two girls of my batch, discussing the weekly schedule of classes pasted on the college notice board.

Monday: 1930-2200 hours: Organizational Behaviour: Faculty name- Prof. R. Siddique.

Classes scheduled that late in the night hit Vandana Mishra like a hard, rude shock.

'Are they crazy or something? Night shift classes or what? I hope this is just a prank being played on us by some seniors!'

'Face the reality, babes!' replied Soha Sharma. 'This pretty much *is* our actual class schedule. And it's gonna remain something like this for the coming two years.'

'You psyche me out Soha! Back home, I don't think I would have stayed up beyond 10 a single night, save under exceptional circumstances like a cousin's wedding or something. If our class here ends at ten, when do I eat, and then when do I sleep!'

'Welcome to Mumbai, darling!' said Soha. 'Mumbai is different from Nainital, and you got to accept the change.' She had a very prominent vanity about being a Mumbaikar. She spoke with a "been there, done that" air of self-pompousness. 'But what's worse is our Sunday afternoon lecture at twelve. Now *that's* something I consider heartless and inconsiderate.' Soha continued. 'What happens to my late Saturday night fiestas at The Lounge? It takes me till Sunday noon just to come out of my hangover!'

'Hangover?' Vandana gave her a quizzical look.

'Yeah, the usual.'

'You drink?'

'Well, what's the matter? You sound like I told you I just launched a rocket into outer space!'

'Do your parents know about it?'

'Ha ha!!!' Soha went into a roar.

'Was there something so funny I said?' Vandana asked, visiblv offended.

'No sweets, it's just that you need to understand a thing or two. And you will- don't worry. Just give yourself some time!'

'Well, I don't know…'

'But I do. And as far as your sleep cycle is concerned, I'll set that right from today itself.'

'What?'

'There is a theme party happening at The Lounge tonight. I am taking you there. No ifs and buts! And yeah, there are going to be some real hot guys too!'

'Well, some incentive, huh?'Vandana grinned. 'Ok, we'll have it your way. For now, let's go have lunch.'

As they entered the canteen, we were still at our table, discussing the recently concluded India-Pakistan one day series. I watched as Sameer went "Sourav Ga.....ga...ga....", and then continued going gaga from the moment he noticed Soha. The waiter came to our table to take further orders, but Sameer seemed to remain absolutely oblivious.

'How much for the French fries?' I asked.

'Rs. 14.'

'Ten!' Sameer exclaimed.

'No boss, 14 means 14. There is no bargaining here.'

'Not you *baba*, I am talking about the rating I would give to that Miss Perfect who has just walked in!'

The waiter looked nonplussed, and his face flushed a ruddy red colour. 'On second thoughts, just let it be, boss! I think I am through with my meal.' I said.

Sameer now had his concentration entirely focused on the girls who had just walked in- a concentration as intense as my mother would have wanted me to have when I studied Social Studies chapters in my primary classes. Soha walked towards the counter, dressed in dangerously low waist denim of a monkey crush blue, and a fuchsia tank top with a plunging neckline. The print on the top said, "Kiss me before my boyfriend comes back", which spoke oodles of her attitude. She sported a cute little navel ring, which caught the attention of every single guy sitting in there. Her gait had a definite mark of flirtatiousness, which had Sameer completely bowled over.

'C'mon, let's go meet her.' he said.

'I am not too sure, Sameer. Our class starts in the next ten minutes.'

She's got an attitude Sameer, knock it off. She's going to shoo us away.

'We'll be quick alright! We need to know our colleagues, don't we?'

'Ok, let's go.'

I know we need to mingle with the chicks fast. So you've also observed the 4:1 proportion, huh?

We walked across to their table, Sameer leading from the front.

'Hi! I am Sameer. I saw you in the class this morning, but I don't think I met you.'

'I bet you didn't,' Soha replied. 'I was not present for the morning class.'

Hit Wicket! Things couldn't have begun worse for him. Poor S.B!

'Oh, no wonder! I could have kicked myself otherwise, for having missed a face as beautiful as that!'

Soha burst into a mischievous laughter. 'Not a bad opening line at all- pretty interesting, I must say! Anyway, I am Soha Sharma. I am a local, so you can get in touch with me for anything you need to know about Mumbai.'

Sameer jumped at the chance. 'Oh cool! I've actually been looking for a few day scholars in our batch who could show me around the city. This is my first time in Mumbai. So do you think you could take me out tonight? Maybe Gateway or something?'

'Not tonight, dear!' *Hmm, surely a line Sameer would never want to hear from a girl.* 'But I'll let you know soon. By the way, guys, this is Vandana.' Soha gestured.

'Hi, how are you?' Vandana said, rather softly. We had barely begun to answer her questions and get a discussion rolling, when she quietly excused herself from the group and walked away. Her coyness could have initially been conveniently mistaken for snootiness, but I refrained from making inferences. I had concluded over a period of time that the lesser you try and analyze girls, their moods and their behaviour, the more convenient and uncomplicated your life becomes.

The bell went off, signaling the end of the recess. But Sameer apparently hadn't heard it. He was still going great guns in his effort to woo Soha, though it was very difficult to decide who the wooer was and who was the wooed. Aryan, Swapnil and I moved up to the classroom, and Sameer told us that he would join us in "a minute or two."

CHAPTER 3

Why MBA?

My hostel room was located in the B-wing of the residential block, on the third floor. The room was pretty decent, or at least, better than what I had expected it to be. It was not a matchstick sized enclosure as I had pictured in my mind. The room was airy, and had a fulsome view of the skyscrapers that touched the skies of suburban Mumbai. The domestic airport was in close vicinity of our institute, and every few minutes, one could hear the burring sound of a jet flying over our building.

There were two beds put up in the room, each of them covered with newly purchased bed sheets. Beneath one of the beds lay a giant sized V.I.P suitcase, and an airbag, half unzipped. There were two small idols of Lord Ganesha and Lord Krishna, on the window sill behind this bed. I made a minute assessment of the room, to check for all the possible stuff that I would need to buy from the market. I made a long list that looked like:

- ❑ Door mat
- ❑ Hand wash
- ❑ Phenyl bottle

- ❑ Naphthalene balls
- ❑ Biscuits
- ❑ Mineral Water....

I didn't have much company then, as my roommate was out. So I decided to walk down to the market, buy the items I needed, and also do a bit of exploring. The hallway was nearly empty, except for a few guys sitting on the parapet discussing their experiences of the first day, or some of them sitting in a corner, smiling away to glory on the phone, apparently talking to their girlfriends. Most of them were in their rooms, and the hostel was almost completely silent, except for the occasional sounds of hard rock escaping a few half-open doors of some rooms.

At the exit gate of the hostel I was stopped by a hugely built, grumpy looking security guard. The sternness on his face, clubbed with his dense moustache and tobacco-stained teeth had the potential to scare the life out of anyone. He looked straight out of one of those characters of the Enid Blyton stories, monsters who were appointed to guard haunted mansions against nosy kids who wanted to peek around.

'Where are you going?' he asked in a baritone voice.

'I am going to the market to buy a few things for my room.'

'First year?'

'Yes.'

'*Sign karne ka.*' *You got to sign.* He pulled out a fat register and handed it to me.

The details required to be filled in were of epic length. The column looked something like:

Sr. no.	Name	Course (Full time/Part time/ Family business)	Out time	Reason for going out	Expected time of return	Sign.

'Don't miss the deadline,' he warned. 'Else you will have to spend the night outside.' 'Alright.'

I fumed. Was this some kind of a boarding school? And if this was our plight, what would be the condition of the girls in their hostel? Would the guard there escort each girl whenever and wherever she went?

The development in Juhu would arguably be the dream location for anyone to buy or build a house. There is a calm, peaceful feeling about the whole area, as it is off the main road, and is hence away from the typical Mumbai traffic and noise. The houses here can be classified into row houses, apartments and mansions. While the row houses and apartments are also very impressive, they are still the normal, routine kinds I got to see in Chandigarh. But the mansions had a very magnanimous appearance, something that I had either imagined in the fairy tales I read in my childhood, or what I had seen in the movies. These houses had huge walls built around them that did not allow us to see much. But on the few occasions when the gate was open, one could catch a glimpse of the excellent architecture, creepers and *bougain-villas* sensuously twined around the building, beautiful gardens in the front view, laden with scores of variety of flowers and plants, and a wide porch that had, at any given time, at least a couple of swanky cars, that would be the fancy of any automobile buff. Most of such mansions, I learnt, were the prized possessions of the top notch, page 3 socialites, like film stars, celebrities and industrialists.

The streets of Juhu scheme are abuzz with activity at this time of the evening. Senior citizens are seen marching towards the neighbourhood park for their evening walk with full gusto. College students laze around in bunches and couples, perched atop their cars, smoking out the day's fatigue, and gorging on their favourite *pani puri* and *bhel puri* at the *Bholu Bhel* stall. The vehicular movement is also high at this hour, as executives make their way back home after a long day at their office.

The Juhu market comprises a series of shops that include the regular grocery marts, stationery shops, vegetable and fruit vendors, sweets centers, coffee shops, and what have you of any and everything that you can imagine you might need. The place is boisterous, with a continuous inflow of customers in every shop, shrewish housewives haggling over the price of vegetables, and hawkers beckoning to passers-by to come and have a look at their products.

I bought the items I needed, and began to head back to the hostel. The typical Mumbai humidity was catching up on me, as I found my completely soaked shirt stick to my body like glue. The sky was overcast, but the rains had not begun yet. I had heard that the monsoon in Mumbai was nothing to be joyous about, as most often it led to innumerable peeves like road clogs, epidemics, and very often, the rains were so ruthless that they could bring the entire life of Mumbai to a standstill. But if rains were the solution to this stuffiness in the air, the minor sores that accompanied them were welcome. Or so I guessed.

Back at the hostel gate, the same security guard stopped me once again.

'Where to?' he demanded.

'Inside, obviously!' I retorted.

'Show me your i-card first.'

'What the...,' I was beginning to lose it now. 'I just spoke to you an hour back before going out. Don't you remember?'

'Look here, on an average a person enters or exits this gate every thirty to forty seconds. How can you expect me to keep a tab all the time?'

I sighed. 'Whatever! My i-card is up in my room, I shall carry it with me all the time from now on, can you let me get in this once?'

'Ok,' he said with a tone of authority. 'But take care next time. We have been given strict orders to follow the rules and get them followed.'

I clenched my teeth in rage and made my way up to the third floor. The door of my room was open. I entered to find Swapnil sitting in deep meditative pose in front of the idols of Lord Ganesha and Lord Krishna. I quietly tiptoed in, kept my bag on the table, and waited for him to finish his prayer.

'Hey there!' He spoke after five minutes of silence.

'Hi, so we meet again!'

'Yeah, I didn't know we were allotted the same room.'

'Neither did I. I am pretty satisfied with the arrangements, though.'

'Yeah,' he said, 'they are far better than I had actually expected.'

As we got into a discussion, we discovered our common interests in reading, and we got talking in depth of the numerous novels we had read. We were absorbed into the conversation, and before we knew it, we were called down for dinner.

The dining hall was big enough to hold a wedding reception party. Tables were arranged in four long rows, and covered with white tablecloths. The menu for the evening was ladyfingers, potatoes cooked in some strange concoction of gravy, *dal, jeera* rice, and *rotis* so stretchable that we could hold them from either end and play tug-of-war.

'Look at this!' Sameer said in a tone of exasperation as we stood in a long queue to fill our plates. 'A beeline for this watery element they call *dal*!'

'I can't eat this food!' I winced.

'Ditto!' Aryan said. 'It reeks of some smell I hate. What is it anyway? There's more oil in the bowl than ladyfingers!'

The smell was repellent to say the least. The gravy that we could see was supposed to be *dum aloo,* but the potatoes were missing. Chewing on the semi-cooked *rotis* was an arduous task. The *jeera* rice was the only remotely palatable item on the platter, but there was nothing to mix with it. The *dal* was so thin in its consistency that it merely wetted the rice, without actually forming an edible mixture with it.

'It tastes worse than it smelt,' Sameer said as he contorted his face on serving himself the first bite of *roti* with the spice-laden gravy. 'I'm out of here.'

He got up in protest and began to walk off.

'Hold on, Sameer,' Swapnil called back, 'I've got quite a few packed buns up in the room. They are pretty bland, but might be a tad better than what we have here!'

'You are a saviour!' Sameer beamed. 'Show me the way!'

'Do you have enough buns to feed three hungry stomachs and a monster?' I asked hopefully.

'I don't know about the monster,' Swapnil grinned, 'but there's enough to feed four hungry human stomachs! So come along.'

We carried the buns up to the hostel terrace and began to devour them. The terrace provided a perfect picture of the landscape of suburban Juhu. The top view of all buildings looked like boxes of cement and concrete packed next to each other like cartons in a factory. Above them floated clouds of smoke emanated from the humongous city traffic that impeded a fulsome view of the sea beach at a slight distance. In time to come, the terrace was to be our regular haven for discussing our smallest of problems, for venting out our deepest frustrations, and for celebrating our smallest achievements.

The building right opposite our hostel was an eight-floor apartment. The house on the top floor had the living room exposed to our view. Whoever designed that house definitely had a superb artistic sense. The furnishing of the living room was exquisite, with the best looking upholstery possible, and a giant screen plasma television that completed the look of an elegant drawing room. Some two or three obscure paintings decorated the front wall. I didn't understand art much, but given the obscurity of the paintings, I could safely assume they must have been modern art. A young girl, presumably around thirteen to fourteen years of age, entered the room with a bowl of ice-cream, and sank into the sofa, with her eyes glued to the TV.

'Nah! Those polka dotted shorts don't look good,' Sameer remarked with a tone of utmost sincere advice. 'They are for kids.'

'She *is* a kid, Sameer, come off it now!' Aryan replied. 'At least spare the younger ones.'

'Hey, I am not hitting on her, ok? I just said she shouldn't be wearing polka. The spaghetti straps look cute, though.'

He lit a cigarette and exuded little rings in the air, wearing a poised expression, smug with the perfection with which he assessed girls and the goodness of their fashion. It was too early to know his true success rate when it came to being lucky with them, but the conviction that he showed in his voice when he talked about them was undoubtedly impressive.

'Sameer, do you never think beyond spaghetti straps and plunging necklines?' Swapnil asked sarcastically.

'Heck no!' Sameer rolled his eyes in a gesture of astonishment. 'You're being judgmental. I also give due credit to the halter necks and the tube tops!' He guffawed.

'On a serious note,' Swapnil went on, 'does any topic of discussion other than girls ever stir you up?'

'Well, let's see,' Sameer pondered. 'Ok, let's have your type of discussion.'

'And what would that be?' Swapnil asked.

'You tell me,' Sameer said. 'Maybe something like "Why MBA"?'

'I'm outta here then,' Aryan declared, picking up another bun. 'I've been asked this question several times before, and I hate answering it. There are no answers to all "whys" anyway.'

'I decided on an MBA because I feel it will offer me better job prospects,' Swapnil said. 'My experience of two years in the construction sector could be well leveraged...'

'That's the answer you may have given to the panelists who interviewed you in the admission process,' Sameer argued. 'Tell us the actual reason!'

'This is the actual reason!' Swapnil said defiantly.

All eyes turned to me.

'I don't think I know,' I shrugged, 'maybe I had nothing better to do. Moreover, this was the only way my parents would send me for a two year paid holiday!'

'Listen, this senseless discussion at this time of the night is the maddest thing to do,' Aryan protested. "And now that we are already here and are here to stay, it's pointless figuring out why. So I beg of you not to bug me with this. I'd rather tolerate the debate on polka shorts and spaghetti straps.'

'Good boy!' Sameer smiled. 'That calls for a toast!'

The next four hours into the night were worth putting into our memoirs. Sameer got into his "highs" after downing a few liters of liquor, and then, getting swayed by emotions, began relating his previous affairs in Calcutta, why each one of them failed, and his newfound feelings for Soha. It was almost unbelievable that a girl could emit in a single meeting such strong influence as to get a guy singing her paeans at 1:30 in the night.

'Don't misunderstand me, guys,' said a tipsy Sameer. 'I am no Casanova. I got a heart. It's just that somewhere I have faltered in all three relationships I've had so far. In fact, the third one...Deepa...I really felt for her deeply...actually, maybe I still do.....no, I know that I do...but there's nothing much I can change...I guess destiny always has its way...my blasted destiny...!'

'Sameer, I think you need some sleep. We have a long day awaiting us tomorrow,' Aryan said in a concerned voice.

'Hey, I am not done yet,' Sameer protested. 'Why did it have to happen that way?'

'What happened what way?' I asked.

'Deepa's attitude...it sucked towards the end...I began to feel deprived....there were times when I needed her, but couldn't find her around. You know why? Because she would be busy with her other friends....and her justification would be that she had other commitments to keep...what crap, I must say! And then she complained I was possessive....which I was not...my sole need was that at least a minimum bit of time should have been kept reserved for me....now can you call that being possessive at all?'

'I am afraid that *was* being possessive,' I said cautiously.

'Like bull crap it was...you don't understand...I never questioned her about her other friends...all I wanted was some bit of her time....and when I would ask for it explicitly, she would do it as a mere obligation...things don't work this way *yaar*! I was her boyfriend who rightfully deserved that time from her, not some pigeon in a park she was obligating by feeding... '

He had now reached his peak of inebriation and was ready to throw up anytime. We tried to haul him up and take him down to his room, but he resisted. He rested himself against the parapet of the terrace wall, and began humming something dreamily, till he gradually fell asleep.

'Well, whoever this Deepa was, I don't really blame her,' I said. 'It's naturally difficult to reserve your mind and time space for a single person always. I think it's even wrong to expect so much from someone.'

'Of course not,' Swapnil replied. 'If you are in a relationship, expectations to this extent are a corollary. You cannot dispense with them. I think it was perfectly natural for Sameer to expect this modicum bit from his girl. In fact, I'll tell you what-these expectations are what make every relation sore if you can't cope with them.'

'I don't know,' I said. 'I kind of empathize with Deepa. If someone tries to encroach upon my free space, I will begin to feel suffocated. If you decide to get into a relationship, it is assumed that you should have attained a level of mature understanding between each other. And if that understanding exists, you should be ready to provide some leeway to each other.'

'Try saying that when you get into a relationship,' Swapnil said, 'or for that matter, even when you have just made a very close friend. See if you say the same then.'

'If you're done with your arguments, we can decide what we do with Mr. Lover Boy!' Aryan said, chewing on his umpteenth bun.

'Damn, it's almost three!' I exclaimed

'Yes, and we have an inaugural ceremony starting at nine in the morning. And it starts with an introductory speech by the dean. I don't want to be caught sleeping through it!' Swapnil said.

'Alright then, let's hit bed,' Aryan said. 'So much for an entertaining and knowledge-enhancing group discussion!'

We laughed. 'By the way,' Aryan said, 'did I tell you guys I suck at group discussions? I often wonder how I managed to get in here! And I am already scared about the summer placement process!'

'Don't worry,' I patted him on the back. 'Be with us, and we'll train you well. We are going to have plenty of such rehearsals before the summer placements!'

'Yeah, so, what do we do about Mr. Lover Boy?' Swapnil asked, pointing towards Sameer. He was fast asleep, spread wide on the floor.

'Let's use some muscle!' Aryan said, flexing his humongous biceps.

We heaved Sameer up on our shoulders. His apparently frail structure was a big deception. Carrying him on you would make you feel like a dozen gunny bags thrown on your back.

'Are we going paragliding?' Sameer asked dreamily.

'You bet we are! And trust me, I have never enjoyed it this much!' Aryan retorted.

CHAPTER 4

Impossible is Nothing

Getting up and ready at seven-thirty in the morning was never going to be easy after barely four hours of sleep. Not for someone who was habituated to eight hours of uninterrupted sleep until then. Not for someone whose bed creaked loudly with the smallest twist or turn at night. Not for someone who was kissed goodnight by pesky mosquitoes every thirty seconds. And definitely not for someone who knew that the reason he had to get ready was to go attend some function, which comprised a series of lectures offering some unsolicited *gyan*, sermon, about what responsibilities lay ahead of us as future corporate czars.

I lay groggily in bed, hoping that Swapnil would occupy the bathroom before me, thus giving me an excuse to catch up on some more sleep. But Swapnil was still asleep, or at least pretended to be, and probably expected me, in turn, to get ready first. I finally relented, and dragged myself to the bathroom. Fifteen minutes before we were to leave, Swapnil was still in bed. I woke him up angrily.

'Swapnil, do you know what time it is?'

'Yeah. It's eight thirty.'

'And what time do we have to get there?'

'Nine. Don't worry, we'll be there five minutes before time. I have all the calculations worked out already.'

'Very well, can you explain?'

'It will take me five minutes to explain this to you, and then ten minutes for me to get ready. The venue for the function is a ten-minute drive from our hostel in a rickshaw. This means we'll be there at eight fifty-five!'

'Good. Now let me see you get ready in ten minutes.'

True to his word, Swapnil was out in exactly seven minutes, wearing a triumphant smile on his face.

'How the hell did you manage that?' I asked in disbelief.

'I saved on the time you took to take a bath.' He smiled.

'You mean you didn't take a bath!' I cringed.

'Of course I did. I believe in hygiene. But I took a shower last midnight. I call it time management. I bathed for yesterday as well as for today!'

I was too stumped to respond. This was an out-of-the-world case of time management, and it was difficult to say whether it was worthy of admiration or of reprimand. But whatever it was, it kept him punctual, and that's what ultimately mattered. He then dedicated the balance three minutes to his morning prayer. The sincerity showed on his face each time he closed his eyes and bowed down in front of the deity. And while I was devout too, I know I never prayed with that passion of a hermit. Maybe somewhere at the back of my mind I was conscious that being explicit in one's devotion would not pretty much fall in line with the mindset of my age and generation. But this guy was absolutely unfazed and unperturbed by what happened around him. When he prayed, it was like he attempted to be one with the Almighty, in full gratitude for whatever had been bestowed upon him. And his sincerity was admirable.

At sharp eight forty-five, we got into a rickshaw.

'S.J Hall. Make it quick,' I said.

The rickshaw driver put on his music speakers that played some corny B grade number containing some obnoxious lyrics. I felt sick. Where were all the Naushads and Khayyams of yesteryears? To add to the sore, the music was loud enough for the whole of Vile Parle to listen to and savour the insane melody of the lyrics.

'Boss, reduce the volume!' I screamed.

'No!' pat came the reply.

'What the...! Look at the cheek of the man!'

'Chill,' Swapnil said. '*Bhaiya*, why don't you reduce the volume, please?'

'Because it can't be reduced,' he replied coldly. 'Volume knob is broken.'

'Then shut the damn thing off.' I begged.

'Ok, after this song. I like it.'

Thanks! That quite serves my purpose.

After ten minutes of deafening torment, we reached the venue. We reached the gate to find that we were two of the earliest to arrive.

'Was my watch too fast?' I asked, surprised.

'No, it's just that you ignored one known fact,' Swapnil said with a triumphant smile, 'that however late you are, there will still be people who will come in after you!'

Roughly half an hour later, streams of students started pouring in. Most of them wore formal shades of blue and white, except some who donned the pinks and purples. The faculty members began to enter only after nine thirty, followed by the dean, who came out of his sexy Lexus at nine forty-five. We were all handed a card which read the day's schedule. Compulsively, my sight fell on all the recess sessions.

10:30–10:45: Tea

12:30–13:30: Lunch

15:45–16:00: Tea

'There are three recesses,' I said gleefully, 'I think I can live through the day!'

'Don't be too hopeful,' Swapnil cautioned, 'I just told you deadlines are hardly followed. The function has not yet begun, which means the first tea break might be scrapped.'

Sadly, he was right. The proceeds of the function began as late as 10:00, with the welcome address delivered by the president of the "Student Activity Group" (SAG) of the senior batch. I had a lame hope that they would curtail the duration of the initial few speeches so as to ensure we got our tea break exactly at ten thirty. But it was a really lame hope.

Excellent! Now we sit through the first two and a half hours, listening to "Responsibilities as a corporate citizen", "How to avoid procrastination", and "Corporate India- A paradigm shift" back to back, and that too without an incentive for tea and comestibles!

We occupied a row far behind, to mitigate the possibility of any of the authorities catching us take a snooze. Not surprisingly, other students thought much like we did, as a result of which the hall had the frontal sixty percent of its seats unoccupied. Sameer sat quietly for a change, as though reflecting upon something with utmost intensity. Matter-of-factly, however, he was not yet out of his hangover of the previous night. He sat with his gaze fixed downwards, and this time he was not checking out any tanned legs for sure.

'Are you OK?' I asked.

'Why did I drink last night? I must've looked like a jerk!' He said abashedly.

'Don't bother about all that, it was just the four of us!'

'Still, I think it was stupid.'

'Forget it now, just tell me are you alright or do you need something?' I was afraid he might want to throw up during the function, and that could create quite a scene.

'No, I am fine. Give me some time. I'll be good.'

The SAG president was still at it, singing praises of the body, and the activities it conducted under the aegis of the institute. 'Dear friends, I seek your support and enthusiasm in the smooth functioning of the SAG...We are here for a cause....I assure you that the SAG will fulfill this cause, and also give you something to cherish for a lifetime...If there is any problem you face, however trivial, remember that your seniors will be just a call away...[*Sniff!!!!!*]...I'll now hand over the dais to our dean, Mr. Anil Mehra.'

Even as he invited the dean over to the mike, he refused to leave the dais. He stood still, staring at a blank-faced audience, in candid anticipation. After a few moments of silence, the crowd clapped, exactly five times. Formality completed. He heaved a sigh of relief, wore a smug look, and then made way for the dean.

'My dear students, I cordially welcome you to our family!' Mr. Mehra began with an emotion-packed statement that would give all the schmaltzy Indian family drama movies and TV soaps a run for their money. 'I know this might be a period of anxiety for all of you as you stand on the threshold of your career.....remember, impossible is nothing.........perseverance and dedication are the key to all forms of success.......' . He went on for no less than thirty minutes, and the pain in my sleepy eyes was getting intolerable. It's not that the speech was soporific. In fact, he was damn good. He spoke in a tone that commanded respect, a speech that contained no-nonsense material, and an excellent gift of the gab. And moreover, he drove a sexy Lexus. He had made it big in life, and definitely had to be a man of substance. But my bodily energy was zilch, and my mind refused to take in anything that he said.

He continued: 'Competition is stiff.......you have to carve a niche for yourself, else you'll be thrown away by the tide.....[*snooze*]......we are definitely in for a better tomorrow, but the onus lies on you-on the youth....[*snooze*]......'. He paused for a while, observed with a very disappointed expression the unoccupied seats in the front rows, and continued. 'I'll also give you a humble piece of advice if you can take it. If you want to move ahead in life, start doing it right away. I urge the students sitting right back out there to come and take the seats ahead...[*snooze*]...'.

I was woken up with a jerk. 'Wake up, Nakul, the dean's asking us to move ahead,' Aryan whispered. This had to be the last straw. Now we would have dozens of watchful eyes on us, making sure we forced ourselves to listen to each word with rapt attention. The next two hours moved on like a drag, with each point being emphasized by each speaker in at least ten different ways. And at the end of it all, there was just so much to be put in a nutshell: "Great opportunities and greater responsibilities await us ahead. Work sharp, work smart. Scale all horizons."

The post lunch session provided no relief. Instead, it only got worse, with the fried rice and cashew-enriched gravy of *malai kofta* adding to our already woeful condition of drowsiness. I took out a novel and began reading. It helped me stay up for some half hour, before Aryan nudged me.

'That faculty's got you!' He hushed.

I turned to look at a grouchy lady, standing akimbo, giving me a petulant look. I froze as I saw her walk up to me. 'Come and meet me after this session ends, young man!' She hissed.

'Just hope that either she doesn't teach us any important subject this trimester, or that she's got a very short memory!' Aryan said.

Six hours and eleven speeches later, I was a tired person. And after sitting through the entire day within the confinements of an auditorium, we felt too claustrophobic to go back to our hostel room.

'Vandana and I are going down town. Why don't you guys join us?' Soha offered.

'Well…' I began.

'Of course,' Sameer cut in, 'you got the words out of my mouth. Let's go.'

'But you weren't feeling well this morning?' Aryan asked with a tone of concern.

'I'm much better now,' Sameer said, stamping hard on Aryan's foot.

'But…'

I saw the grouchy faculty member walk out of the hall with a colleague.

'Let's get out of here and then decide,' I pleaded, 'otherwise I have a second series of lectures for me in the offing.'

CHAPTER 5

Ateneris Impende Laborem

While JVPD scheme gives the view of an elite, top class lifestyle of Mumbai, the local station ofVile Parle offers a more realistic, more holistic picture of the lifestyle of the larger chunk of the city's junta. Come 19:00 hours, and you can see Mumbaikars swarming the station in tens of thousands. Blue and white collared workers are seen returning from a grueling day at office. Whether they have got a raise for the extra hours they have been putting in, or whether they have been rebuked by their boss for not having met their monthly targets, they have put the events of the day behind them, and are eager to get back home, sit comfortably in their snug houses, and spare a moment or two they have reserved for their personal lives. Students from undergrad colleges are trying to rush home soon, because they have to wrack their brains over some data to write that thousand word assignment for their mid-term submissions, with a combined tension due to the forthcoming exams. Hawkers have sold part or whole of their day's stock of fish and vegetables in the market, and are going back to their chawls to try and manage the day with their spoils. These local trains of Mumbai are known to be a vehicle where all these people with myriad backgrounds meet, share their daily experiences with one another, try and divide their despair between each other, and end up making new friends- train buddies. By the time they reach their destinations, they have let most of the despair wear off, and have made a resolution to begin the next day with new hope and zeal.

We stood on the platform, waiting for the Churchgate-bound local to arrive. The multitude of people who had thronged the platform, all stood waiting to board the same train.

'How long does the train halt at the station?' Swapnil asked.

'Thirty seconds, approximately,' Soha replied.

That was a formidable challenge. Some four to five hundred people were going to try and squeeze their way through a few narrow doors of the train in less than thirty seconds. And what was worse, most of them looked well trained to do so, unlike novices like us.

'How are we going to manage this?' I asked nervously.

'You need to be agile, that's it.' Soha said, looking me up from head to toe, and letting out a sly smile.

'I'm pretty spunky,' I said agitatedly, 'don't worry about me.'

Spunky I was. I looked around my body, consciously inspecting my anatomical configuration. Alright, so there were some five kilos here and five kilos there that needed to be dispensed with, and some globules of adipose that peeked shyly over my belt region, but that was not going to deter my courage. I stood at the edge of the platform, ready to wade my way through the swarm and lunge onto the train as soon as it arrived.

'We have ten minutes,' Soha said. 'You guys can come and sit here.'

As the six of us took seats on a bench in the centre of the platform, I observed a couple of roadside Romeos, ogling at something in our direction with a conspicuously lecherous glow in their eyes. I traced their line of sight and found the source to be Soha's figure-hugging tight "formal" skirt that had become eye-candy for the onlookers. The skirt as well as her top had all the right cuts at all the right places, and to the pleasure of most, revealed more than what was necessary. And she only enhanced the view by sitting casually on the bench in a cross-legged posture. And while we all fidgeted with embarrassment, Soha looked absolutely unperturbed. Vandana leaned forward and whispered something in her ear, in response to which Soha let out a short laugh.

'It's their problem, baby,' Soha said coolly, 'I am pretty used to this sore of society. I see it happen everywhere. I think beauty comes with a price, doesn't it?' She brushed her fingers lightly through her hair and winked in a gesture of extreme self-pompousness.

Self-praise has little acknowledgment, and most beautiful girls I have always known seldom acknowledge this fact. It was amusing, in fact, almost unbelievable to see the levels of immodesty they nurtured within themselves.

'Now!' Soha shouted in sync with the screech of the train as it pulled to a halt at the platform. Saying so, she charged forward, leading Vandana by the hand, and before we knew it, they had both disappeared. For the next twenty-five seconds or so, we watched people pushing, jumping over one another's head, trying to grab entry into the train before it left for the next destination. I felt almost defeated at the hands of the rowdy jostlers, and was unable to push myself through the anarchic crowd. Out of sheer desperation, I pleaded: 'Excuse me, I want to get in!'

'So? Do you want me to pick you up and put you in?' growled a big bully standing ahead. He turned his back towards me, roughed aside a few weaker souls standing in his way, and then stomped his way inside the compartment.

Thirty seconds later, I gave up the pointless fight and retreated, even as I saw the train chug away from me. As the crowd on the platform dispersed, I saw my three trusted friends standing alongside me on the platform, who had been clearly as unsuccessful in their mission. We looked at one another helplessly, and then burst out laughing. A man standing nearby, who had been watching everything, looked at us and smiled. 'Boss, "excuse me" doesn't work here. You have to push and kick hard, else you'll keep standing here through the night.'

'Where are the girls?' I asked.

'They boarded the train. It's much simpler in the ladies compartment,' replied Sameer. 'Even we should have got in there!'

'Yeah, right!' Aryan mocked. 'And have our *mama* waiting for us at the next platform to take us for a visit to his cell!' *Mama* is a typical Mumbai slang that means one of the several cops who stand at traffic signals, local stations and other such locations where they can find miscreants and nail them.

Sameer laughed. 'Anyway, Soha just messaged they will meet us at Churchgate at the exit gate.'

'We had better work our way through this crowd this time,' Swapnil warned.

We moved to the edge of the platform, leaning over every few seconds to see any signs of the train arriving. When it finally did, we charged ahead, with a firmer resolve to make it. Like four warriors, we sprang forward. Collars were pulled, punches were placed, people pushed and tugged around with full might, climbing over one another, trying to scamper into the train. Braving the hurdles, we somehow managed to get in. But the condition inside the train was not great either. People stood stuck to one another like glue, stepping on one another's shoes, breathing out hot air on one another's faces, dropping their sweat on one another's clothes. Many of them stood dangling near the open door, with half their body swaying to the outside precariously. Getting a seat was a distant dream; we had no option but to stand like four wax statues. No bodily movement was possible, except when the train would halt at each subsequent station. Irrespective of whether we had to get down there or not, we would involuntarily be pushed outwards onto the station by the stream of people trying to disembark. Then, once again, would begin the laborious effort at trying to embark again onto the train, this time with a new unruly crowd.

Amidst this crazily crowded compartment, a young boy, all of twelve or thirteen, dressed in tattered rags, tried to walk his way through, with his little sister trailing behind him. He had a handful of incense sticks with him, which he had to sell to earn the day's bread for both of them. But the flock of people around him was too busy and tired to even notice him. He shouted and pleaded at the top of his fawn-like voice, but to no avail. Swapnil finally beckoned him to come over, and bought two incense sticks for five rupees. They would come handy in his morning prayers. Five rupees seemed enough to light up a look of satisfaction on the lad's face. While I do not advocate any form of begging or child labour, sometimes it would be worthy enough to step into his shoes, and try and feel his angst. And I knew I mostly could not feel it. Most of us mostly cannot feel it.

Forty minutes later, we breathed fresh air as we alighted at Churchgate station. We met Soha and Vandana at the exit gate.

'Bozos, we've been waiting almost an hour! How could you be so clumsy as to not get in?'

'It was a mad rush out there, don't ask!' Aryan wailed, as he tried to stretch his back that had got stiffened from the arduous journey.

'Let's walk!' She said.

'Where are we eating?' Vandana asked.

'I don't care where,' I said, 'just make it fast. And it should not be a very long walk!'

'Don't worry,' Soha said, 'it's down the road.'

We walked down to Gaylord's, a restaurant that stood hardly hundred feet from the station gate. The ambience of the restaurant looked like it fitted my taste to the T. But a sneak peek into the prices on the menu card changed my opinion. They were the kind of prices that could not be afforded by students like us, who planned to thrive on watertight budgets while staying away from home. It was different in Soha's case; one because she was a local, and two, because she could easily get away with a free dinner, using a little cute flutter of her eyelashes in front of Sameer.

The food, though, was appetizing, and a welcome change from the insipidness that marked the hostel cuisine. We wolfed down the food as it came, and ate religiously till our bellies could take in no more.

'That was nice!' Aryan moaned, as he stretched himself after a hearty meal.

'And the bill's even nicer!' I quipped, as I saw the gargantuan total of Rs. 1940 stare into my face. Dividing it among six meant a 320-plus per head charge. With a heavy heart, we reached for our wallets to bring out our share on the table. As Soha began to open her bag slowly, Sameer raised his hand and stopped her.

'Let it be,' he smiled, wearing the sweetest smile that he could possibly adorn.

Strangely, Soha did not show an iota of resistance as would normally be expected. Instead, she smiled broadly with a twitch of her nose, and pulled Sameer's cheek hard.

'So sweet!' She said in a highly affected tone.

'Wow, Sameer, you are a true pal!' Aryan seized an opportunity as he stuffed his wallet back into his pocket. 'I didn't know you were treating us!'

'Thanks, chum!' I concurred, keeping my wallet back too.

Sameer stuttered. 'No, I only meant...' His face contorted into a livid expression even as we savoured a sadistic moment of pleasure and a free dinner at his expense.

'Ok, done,' Swapnil said, patting Sameer on the hand, 'but next time it will be us, ok?'

'Yeah sure, why not!' Sameer hissed through his tightly clenched teeth.

'You really shouldn't have, Sameer,' Vandana said in complete earnest, '1940 is a huge amount. What's the occasion anyway?'

'I...just felt like...' Sameer mumbled helplessly as he slammed his credit card on the bill. We all looked at one another and smiled. All except Sameer. He had paid a heavy price for his chivalry towards Soha: Rs.1940, to be precise. The only substantial benefit he gained from his unintended act of altruism was that Soha found the free dinner to be the perfect reason to agree to his request to take her out for dinners in the future.

We walked along the Queen's Necklace at Marine Drive for the next hour. The entire drive was lit up with halogen lights, delivering an extremely picturesque view. It was the perfect place to sit and unwind after a hard day's work, a perfect hangout zone for young collegians, and a perfect spot where newly-formed couples could find a cozy moment to share. And it was, of course, the perfect place for nonplussed souls like me, to do a little self-introspection, and try and establish a mission in life. For the two years ahead, I was to find solace by the sea every time I needed it. I always believed the sound of the waves crashing against the rocks, and the zephyr that filled the surrounding would give me the right ambience for a bit of self-reflection. But as it would turn out each time, I would return as confused as before, the zephyr being the only thing stuffing my head.

'What's our schedule for tomorrow?' I asked, as we headed back towards Vile Parle after midnight.

'Regular classes begin tomorrow. We have three of them back to back, one of which is Financial Management!' Swapnil looked at me and smiled, waiting for me to wince and moan.

Regular classes begin from tomorrow... Time to step up some gas, I decided. I entered my hostel room, took out a square piece of paper, a sketch pen, and wrote in gigantic fonts: "You are a bright star. You will shine today. ATENERIS IMPENDE LABOREM." I thrust the paper into an empty frame, and placed it by my bedside.

CHAPTER 6

I haven't Read A Word So Far

Learning the concepts of Financial Management was never going to be easy for a student who had no inclination towards numbers whatsoever, and who had absolutely no idea what a balance sheet looked like.

'How many of you have studied Accounts before, at whatever level?' was the first question Prof. Biswas posed in front of the class of hundred. Roughly forty hands went up instantly. 'Well, that's a much better number than I had expected! This batch seems to have a healthy proportion of commerce graduates. So I presume I can run through the basics a little fast, am I right?' I felt queasy. I hoped someone would stand up and protest, but nobody did. And I did not want to be the only dumb coot to raise my hand.

'For the uninitiated,' he continued, 'I am sure your friends will always be ready to help you out with the basics. And of course, my door is always open for you whenever you need help.'

He ran through a brief explanation of the contents in a balance sheet at the speed of a blitzkrieg. By the time I could draw the balance sheet table in my book, scribble on top "Assets and Liabilities", and try and make sense of whatever Prof. Whirlwind Biswas said, he had already moved on to "Calculation of P/E ratio" and some half-dozen other ratios with it. I felt miserable and hopeless, and began to peep into the notebooks of students around me, hoping desperately to find a lead that could get me going. While there were some beginners who looked as clueless as I was, most others were pretty much in tandem with the pace of the professor. There was this girl in particular, sitting right beside me, who seemed to be pretty adept at this stuff, even as she brought on rapid-fire solutions to every question the professor shot at the class. She wore the look of an intellectual geek; her hair was loosely put up together to make a ponytail that looked like a tree in the tropical Savannas, and she had thin-rimmed glasses perched on her nose.

'Hold on, please!' I said, as she was about to flip the page to solve the next sum. I desperately started copying the entire solution, hoping to try and comprehend it later. She looked up at me, studied me for a moment with a stern look, and then dug back into her sums.

'I am actually an engineer, haven't heard of all this before. Sounds like Greek and Latin to me!' I said, letting out a sheepish smile.

'Uh-huh, I see,' she muttered without looking up, typing furiously into her calculator and continuing her calculations.

Such a cold response would have put off anyone, but something told me I would need her help, so I decided to be more patient.

I continued, 'But it looks like it's a piece of cake for you! I am really impressed!'

'It's hardly something to be impressed about, this has got to be a piece of cake for any and everyone,' she said even more tersely. 'Finance can be very nasty; this is just a warm-up session.'

This was par my tolerance limits. I was scandalized enough already, and to top it, the chick had the gall to show me my actual place with respect to the depth of the subject. I looked at her with slight disdain for her unwarranted arrogance, but she nonchalantly went on with her calculations. I checked out the identity card hung around her neck.

NAME: Naina Rai

DATE OF BIRTH: 19-6-1980

Her seniority in age by three years suggested that she had come with loads of industry experience, and would possibly consider it a wasted investment of time to mingle around with fledglings like me. I got back to my half-hearted effort at comprehending those strange equations and ratios. As she finished her last sum, I was still at the second, trying to fish out the right answer somehow. But I was far from it. She reclined comfortably in her seat, clucking her knuckles in a gesture of accomplishment. After a couple of minutes of watching me struggle, she leaned forward, looked into my notebook, and said, 'You've not factored in the ten percent depreciation.'

'Oh, of course! That explains it all!' I said weakly, as though I knew what depreciation really was, or what it was supposed to be doing in that solution. She realized I followed nothing. She took my notebook, scribbled down each step systematically, writing beside each step the reason for that step, and handed the book back to me.

'Here, I think it should be easier now?'

Like hell it is!

'Well, yeah, thanks!' I said, still confused.

'I am going to be in the library from six to eight this evening,' she continued. 'If you have any more queries you can ask me then. Otherwise it's just going to get tougher progressively.' My severe ineptness in the subject, and in any and everything related to it, had probably become very evident to her.

Lectures on Organizational Behaviour and Marketing Management that followed after, looked as smooth sailing as prose and poetry after three hours of Financial Management. The best thing about them was that there was nothing perfectly right or entirely wrong in there. No lousy equations, no lengthy calculations; just the ability to exhibit creative writing talent was what was needed to drive your point through. I was always reasonably proficient at hurling jargon, reiterating one point in a dozen different ways, and ending up showing at least ten times more than what I actually knew.

At the end of the first day's classes, we had three caselets and one case study in Organizational Behaviour, one presentation on Marketing Management, and two mammoth assignments in Financial Management to submit in the following week. And all these would be graded as mid-term submissions. *Take them really seriously,* our seniors had warned, *don't let them screw around with your internals.*

I sat in the library for most of that evening after classes, trying to chart out a plan to combat the volley of assignments I was assailed with. I spread out a weekly plan on a piece of paper, neatly noting down the timelines I would make myself follow. It was a wasted effort, I knew from experience, to prepare timelines, because the only time I adhered to them was when I made them for the first time in class two or three. Yet, preparing timelines always gave me a fleeting but strong sense of satisfaction that I was willing to commit myself to studying hard.

The next step in attaining that satisfaction was to browse a handbook given to us in class, which was to be used as a reference journal to prepare our assignments. I scanned the contents in order to derive references for my work, and before I could decide to go further, I was greeted by a slap on the back. Aryan and Sameer stood behind me.

'Already?' Aryan asked, raising his brows. 'We have a week to go man! Don't freak me out!'

'I'm not doing much,' I said, 'just waiting for Naina. I am sitting extra classes with her to understand what Mr. Biswas ranted off at jet speed in today's class.'

'Who's Naina?' Aryan asked.

'From our class,' I replied, 'one smart girl she was. You should have seen her solve those numericals this morning!'

'Leave this aside for now,' Sameer cajoled, 'we are planning to go to this pub called Enigma. In any case there is no point beginning to study so early. I haven't read a word so far.'

'Nor have I,' Aryan chipped in, 'and nor will you.' He closed my book and tried pulling me out of the chair.

I haven't read a word so far. The quintessential lie that every single student, in every single phase of his academic career, tells every single colleague he comes across. There is no ulterior motive behind saying so. Yet everyone feels compelled to say it each time he is asked about how well he is prepared for the upcoming exams.

'I'll pass,' I said, 'anyway I don't drink.'

'You can at least give us some company,' Sameer said, 'I'm sure it would be better than sitting through the evening with a nerdy Finance whiz.'

We heard the clearing of a throat and turned around. Naina stood right behind Sameer and Aryan, waiting for them to clear the aisle between two rows they had blocked. She strode past them with marked élan, shooting stern glares at Sameer as she walked by. She came and sat beside me, and flung her shoulder bag onto the table.

'Do you want me to teach you, Nakul, or do you have other commitments?' She asked.

'Guys, *this* is Naina,' I said. 'These are my friends, Sameer and Aryan.'

'Nice,' she said, rather curtly, still giving Sameer the hard glare.

'Hey, I was just kidding,' Sameer said. 'That nerdy thing that I just said...'

Naina's solemn expression suddenly gave way to a munificent smile. It was an impressive, warm smile.

'Relax, you weren't entirely wrong,' she laughed, 'I am a bit of a nerd, depending on how you define the word.'

'We plan on going to the pub,' Aryan said, 'would you like to join us?'

'I would have loved to,' she said, 'especially because I learnt from my roommate that one of you large-hearted guys loves treating his friends! But today I am tied up.'

'Aw jeez,' Sameer wailed, 'you are Vandana's roommate, is it?'

She nodded.

'And she told you what happened at Gaylord's that night!'

She nodded again, this time with a wide grin.

'Well, in an attempt to cover up the losses incurred that night because of my dear friends, I have decided to shun my large-heartedness for now,' Sameer snarled, casting wicked glances at Aryan and me. 'But you can join us sometime nonetheless.'

'Sure,' she said.

'Nakul, are you coming with us or has the knowledge bug bitten you?' Aryan asked.

'It's not a bug,' I said, 'It's a phantom that has scared me and I need to set it right. But I'll get done with this and join you in a bit. You carry on till then.'

'You're the boss,' he said. 'Bye, Naina.'

'Bye.'

'Alright, let's get it rolling,' I said with a deep sigh once Aryan and Sameer left, 'let's begin with its A-B-C!'

'Before the A-B-C you need to note one more thing,' Naina instructed, 'if you view it as a phantom right from the word "go", the entire exercise will be of no use. So be positive.'

'Sure.'

Be positive must be the most hackneyed of all phrases across all spiritual sermons, scriptures and "beautify your life" courses, but she said it with such a tone of authority that I felt compelled to nod my head dutifully in acknowledgement. That I could never implement the policy when it came to understanding or studying Financial Management was another matter. But I was moved by her commitment to the cause.

She sat with me for over an hour, beginning with the very basic fundamentals of the subject, and progressing slowly up to the point where Mr. Biswas had taught in class. I did manage to understand from her that evening the meaning of assets and liabilities, and the motive behind preparing a balance sheet. Beyond that, the positive outcome of that session seemed minimal to me then. What I did not realize then was that the session, and similarly many others that followed prior to our first end-term exams, would germinate within me the recognition of a newfound friendship that ended up defining a large part of me in the following two years.

'If I crack this one, you deserve a big treat!' I promised her.

'Well, if that's the case, I'll ensure you crack it!' Naina chuckled. 'But I will recommend you go through the ratio analysis once again. It will take some time before it sinks in well.'

'I'll do that tomorrow now,' I said, as I prepared to leave. 'I've had today's dose!'

The "tomorrow" stretched to a distant date- something like a day before the end term exam of Financial Management. And the consequences would be very obvious.

CHAPTER 7

Juhu Chowpatty—and The First Rain

The first shower of the season is always a joyous moment, as we seek respite from the blaze of the summers. While we were certainly too old to play with paper boats, we had a picnic of our own. The college authorities showed healthy spirit by calling off the classes for the day. At around four-thirty in the evening, we set out for a *parikrama* of the city on foot. The rain had eliminated the stuffiness in the air, the temperature had dipped, and a cool breeze filled the air. Dressed in ragged shorts and worn out tees, we moved around aimlessly in the by-lanes of Juhu, like a band of gypsies. The walk to Juhu beach was a good twenty minutes from our hostel, and there was still a slight drizzle. Such occasions are rare, where one has little worry for tomorrow, totally oblivious to the ordeal that may lie ahead- just reveling in an eternal moment with the company of three friends, and a lovely weather complementing the setting.

Juhu Chowpatty had a deserted look early in the evening. There was a small group of street urchins playing cricket in one far corner, and a few odd couples romancing under the highly overcast sky. The sea was wild, and huge waves crashed against the shore angrily every few seconds. The atmosphere had enveloped us into an entirely new domain, getting us deviated from our regular, run-of-the-mill discussions on college affairs. It provided us the perfect point to discover one common interest that Aryan and I shared- music. For me, music was but a medium to relax my nerves when they needed it, something like a single panacea for all sores. But for Aryan, it was the essence of life. He said that he thrived on music. It was his comrade in good and bad times alike.

'I have found an ideal ally in music over time,' he always said. 'It is one friend that has always stood by me when I've felt lonely in a crowd. There can't be a more selfless friend!'

This would, prima facie, sound like a sermon being delivered by a recluse, and for a long time I felt so too. But my experiences in time to come made me connect well with all the philosophical matter Aryan spewed.

During those initial months, however, I could not connect well with those thoughts of a recluse. All I knew then was that I had a passion for singing, and needed a mere excuse like an awesome weather to initiate a jamming session- even if our only audience was a handful of stray dogs lurking around on the beach, growling every now and then when my voice broke into a cacophonous pitch.

The rhythm continued to flow through the evening, until it was disrupted by Sameer's noisy ring tone. He walked to a corner, and came back grinning from ear to ear after a brief chat.

'It was Soha,' he said, waving his phone. 'She wants to go shopping, and she doesn't have company.'

'So she has called you?' I asked, raising an eye-brow. For no strong reason, I felt a slight disdain for Soha. Notwithstanding her ultra-hot looks and an extra-sugary voice, her eyes and body language somehow strongly reeked of selfishness and deceit. My interactions with her had been too few for me to have made an objective assessment. But certain inferences about people could be drawn straight from the gut, and this was just one of them.

Sameer nodded. 'Yeah, she has called me. I ought to get going.'

'She has not called you, Sameer,' Aryan said, without shifting gaze from his strings as he tried to grasp the chords of a new song, 'it's your credit card she has called for.'

'That's preposterous!' Sameer protested. 'We are friends, and...'

'And you are in love with her, aren't you?' Swapnil cut in.

'Ah, well,' Sameer blushed, his cheeks and ears forming hues of red and pink, 'not exactly...'

'You mean you are!' Swapnil insisted.

'Well, maybe, yes.' Sameer murmured.

Aryan and I looked at each other with an expression of amusement mixed with astonishment.

'Sameer, you hardly know her yet,' I tried explaining. 'Do give yourself some time before you think on those lines.'

'Everything we think and feel is not a function of time, Nakul,' Sameer said, wagging his head in dissent, 'it just happens, and you've got to let it happen.'

'Does she feel the same way about you?' I asked carefully, trying not to encroach upon his privacy or to influence his emotions. But the thought that he could, in such a short span of time, develop such a strong sense of affection for someone, did not register well with my sensibilities then.

'Should I care?' Sameer asked with a half-smile. 'I can't force her to feel the same way. I feel a certain way, and that's all I need to know. Isn't this how love really is defined?'

'You win, mate!' Aryan raised his hands in a gesture of defeat. 'Now get going, your chick must be waiting for you!'

As Sameer walked away, a temporary silence gripped our surroundings. Nobody spoke anything. Aryan stayed engrossed in trying to get the chords of the next song right, while Swapnil was busy fiddling with his mobile. I permitted myself the luxury to spin into a series of thoughts, trying to find the answer to Sameer's question. *How is love really defined?* To me it meant a feeling of closeness I felt towards someone, to an extent that all my actions, words and beliefs revolved around that one person. Someone for whom I would be prepared to transcend all kinds of hurdles just to ensure a smile on his or her face. Be it in any form of relationship, this common definition held true in my mind. Then again, that meant I would need time to judge if the person was worthy of such sincere love. In view of this definition, then, I could not bring myself to believe that developing such a feeling was not a function of time.

Aryan finally got the chords right, and once again we got back to singing. He strummed John Denver's *You Fill Up My Senses*, and I joined him in chorus, allowing my thoughts to fizzle out in the melody of the soulful rendition.

We were in for a rude shock when we returned to the hostel past midnight. As an apt example of an anticlimax after the heartening experience of the first rain, we found our room playing host to a gang of monstrous mosquitoes and strange-looking insects. The wall had formed gashes at various points, letting in streamlets of water. Chunks of cement had scraped off the otherwise neatly plastered walls, rendering an ugly appearance to the room. Our beds were damp, and the sheets emitted a humid stench. The next three months would make us realize that monsoons in Mumbai were nothing much to exult over. The season stretched longer than we could imagine, playing foul by inflicting a series of ailments in our batch. Sun rays would peep out in a tease, once in some ten or fifteen days, for a guest appearance, before black clouds would loom over again. We had to contain ourselves most of the time within our hostel or our classrooms. The only things that continued giving us respite during those dark, gloomy days were Aryan's guitar and my insatiable hunger for music.

End-term exams for the first trimester came round the corner, and we were yet to begin studying. The oft heard of "pressure and rigour" of an MBA course suddenly started making its presence felt, as we fought against time to try and complete our endless list of pending assignments, mid term exams and presentations in order to ensure we got a presentable grade. I wrote in big, bold letters once again on a piece of paper: START STUDYING TOMORROW, and placed it in the frame by my bedside. *'I will recommend you go through the ratio analysis once again,'* Naina had said. But the little that I had learnt from her had already begun to evaporate into thin air. The horrendously shaped curves of demand and supply in Macroeconomics always left me reeling, and in Statistical techniques, I could not tell the difference between the use of a chi-square test and an ANOVA test. As for the other subjects, I felt I could manage them on the eve of the exam. And it was a very fanciful assumption.

The next morning, I was woken up by a loud, frantic knock on my door. The door was banged loudly at least four times before I managed to pull myself out of bed and drag my feet to the door. Aryan stood outside, looking like there was an emergency.

'Get ready quickly,' he said, 'There is a matinee show of *Sarkar* playing at Globus, Bandra, at ten-thirty!'

'Aryan, are you nuts?' I moaned. 'You didn't have to wake me up for this, did you? The movie can happen anytime.'

'No, it cannot. The tickets for this show are just sixty bucks and it never gets cheaper in Mumbai halls.'

'And do you realize we have our exams in ten days? I know you are as less prepared as I am!'

'Three hours more after two months of laxity won't make one hell of a difference,' he reasoned.

I was prone to giving into temptations, and this one was no exception. Besides the fact that *Sarkar* was the biggest blockbuster during those days, I was a total movie buff, and found it hard to decline an offer for even the shadiest movie around. But those ghoulish images of demand and supply curves continued to haunt me. Moreover, Swapnil and Sameer refused to come because they said they had to start "reading up stuff".

'Are you coming or not?' Aryan shook me hard and asked.

I looked at the frame by my bedside, and read the instruction saying: START STUDYING TOMORROW, and after a moment of silence, said, 'Ok. I'll come.'

CHAPTER 8

Division of Labour

I could not say that I was nervous about the exams. Not because I found myself well prepared, but because I had still not, in full measure, realized what a big soup I was in. I had no idea how well prepared the others were, and I had no idea to what extent the performance of the others would matter to me in this CGPA grading system. My lame efforts began only two days prior to the exams, and that too, was not because some realization dawned upon me, but simply because all the others had themselves dug into their books, and so I had nobody to continue whiling away my time with.

Studying Macroeconomics was like fighting an already lost battle. Two days were never going to be enough to cover fourteen gargantuan chapters, for someone who had just got introduced to the concept of GDP and GNP. I tried to make an assessment of the approximate amount of time it would take me to go through the painful infliction. I counted the number of pages as three hundred and twenty, and kept a deadline of reading and absorbing each page in five minutes. That would give me roughly twenty-seven hours over the two-day span. *Fair enough,* I felt satisfied on seeing my estimate.

But the problem began when I got carried away by the relative simplicity of the first two chapters. I completed the initial forty odd pages in less than two and a half hours, and felt pretty smug after that.

I spent the reserve time that I had saved, in playing *Mario Brothers* on my laptop. When I resumed from chapter three onwards, I found that things were not all that plain and simple anymore. I had transitioned from "What is Macroeconomics", "What are GDP and GNP" to "Understanding demand and supply", "Law of Marginal Utility", and scores of other such terms which left me in a tizzy. Pages that followed showed strange looking figures which were supposed to demonstrate the concept of economic equilibrium, and situations in which this equilibrium could be disturbed. All that I could understand then, was that the equilibrium of my mind was in tremendous tumult. The target of five minutes per page had been breached, and I found myself going tangentially away from the estimate that I had set for myself. What added to my woes was that after a certain point, I seemed to forget everything that I had read previous to that. Consequently, I was forced to revert to the earlier chapters, leaving me stranded at status quo.

After hours of frustration, I walked around the library, looking for someone to accompany me outside for a break. But anyone and everyone who mattered were too busy. Naina, Vandana and Swapnil sat in a far corner, brainstorming animatedly over some topic. Sameer was over at Soha's place, explaining the subject to her from scratch, because she had not attended most of the classes on account of "personal commitments" to keep. Sameer had willingly obliged, as he had, by then, reached a stage where his emotions often overpowered him and got him to digress from his plans in order to make her happy.

The only person who did have as much free time on hand as I did was, as usual, Aryan.

'Let's get out of here,' Aryan said, almost in a whimper, 'this place nauseates me if I sit too long!'

We sat over a cup of coffee, and planned a schedule for the exams.

'Nothing will work unless we strategize,' Aryan declared, assuming a tone of intellect. 'I suggest we split the load between us.'

'Like how, if I may ask?' I questioned.

'Have you heard of division of labour, Nakul? We studied it in basic economics in class 9. We'll split our work for better productivity. I'll do the first seven chapters, and you do the latter seven. Tomorrow we'll explain our respective parts to each other.'

'I don't know, Aryan, I have really not done this before!'

'You haven't achieved anything significant by doing otherwise either, have you?' he smirked.

'Hah! Just about as much as you have, buster!' I said.

Aryan had a knack to convince any and everyone on the face of the earth that his ideas were the best solution to every problem. 'Let's just try it for the first paper. The biggest advantage is that now you don't have to worry about that lousy time calculation per page.'

I finally relented, realizing that I anyway was going nowhere studying alone. We sat down with our Bible-sized books, buried our heads into them for the next five hours, battling simultaneously against boredom, confusion, distraction and time. By dinnertime, we had scribbled notes on dozens of paper sheets, and when we fell short of paper, we began practicing the horrid diagrams on our palms. We felt satisfied with our effort, and decided to treat ourselves to sizzlers for dinner.

We sat at Yoko's Sizzlers that night and made merry like there was no tomorrow. I guess this was the primary reason why I so enjoyed Aryan's company. He seemed to be so much like me, who wanted to live for the day, and was more than willing to put off all worries of the world for tomorrow. We became completely oblivious to the fact that we had our exams two days hence, and that we were likely to get badly screwed. We gorged on our food, discussed everything ranging from spiritualism to music, from past friends to fiction. We sat measuring every chick entering or exiting the restaurant. (In times of desperation, any non-male who did not look like an Amazon qualified as a chick). Our ratings ranged from -15 to 9.99, as we always believed there was room for betterment.

'Have you ever wondered,' Aryan asked, 'What is it about these girls that make us sit up and take notice?'

'Basic law of nature, I guess,' I said. 'But for me it starts and ends at just taking notice. Beyond that it is self-annihilation.'

'Now, now, don't get started with your *gyan* again,' Aryan pleaded. 'I've heard that from you before. But I really want to know what makes you so bitter. Do you have a history you may want to share?'

'Well, if it's a relationship you are hinting at, then no, I have never had one. But even in the normal course of coming across girls, I have found all of them to be kind of weird. They tend to put up a façade most of the time, being something they are really not. You know what I mean?'

'Yeah, I do,' Aryan replied, 'But I think you are generalizing big time here. All girls need not be like that.'

'Well, for me there are only two categories of girls: the girlie girl and the bitchy girl. Take any girl and she will fall into one of these categories!'

'Whoa, now that's something! Would the Lord like to explain?' Aryan mocked.

'The girlie girl is the "Oh-My-God my nail polish has come off" kinds, who is so bloody obsessed with herself that it becomes virtually impossible for her to see sense and logic, or for that matter anything beyond herself. She is solely concerned about how fast her wardrobe gets updated, whether her lip gloss and her mascara are in right measure and right place, and how many guys have gifted her red roses and heart-shaped candies on all Valentine's Days put together. She is on the lookout for the company of guys who can compliment her on her looks every two hours, and who could follow her with her purse in their hands, while she flashes her face in her pocket mirror!'

Aryan laughed. 'And what about the bitchy girl?'

'The bitchy girl is a wily opportunist,' I went on with confidently, 'who makes friends with two primary motives. One, she gets a platform for frivolous gossip mongering, and for slinging mud on every possible person around her-especially other pretty lasses. She misses no opportunity to pick on some person to put down, someone who otherwise does not, even in a minuscule manner, affect her happiness. But she still does it out of sheer force of habit and sadistic pleasure, and revels in company of her "friends" who abet her in such acts of insanity. Secondly, she makes friends only in accordance with the need of the hour. She has no qualms about using people to the extent that they would be useful to her in some way, and after the purpose is served, she discards them.'

'Hmm. That does explain quite a lot, doesn't it?' Aryan said. 'By the way tell me something. In what category would you put Soha?'

Thankfully, I managed to duck the question as the waiter brought the bill on our table right then. '227,' I said, as I brought out my share of the bill. Aryan repeated his question once all was settled.

'I don't know,' I said uneasily, 'what do you think?'

Aryan smiled. 'I think we should leave. It's eleven already!'

We returned to the library and sat again with our books at eleven-thirty, with slight pangs of guilt throbbing at us menacingly, for having let a good deal of time down the drain. I flipped through the first seventy odd pages I had studied a few hours earlier, and to my horror, I realized that I could not recollect a single word from all of that.

'Damn! This is beginning to look alien to me again! I can't remember a single word of what I just learnt!' I cried.

'That's funny, though I feel the same too. Where did it all go?'

'I guess it just evaporated away with the sizzlers!' I began to panic for the first time. 'What do we do now, start from scratch?'

'Don't be crazy. Then when you get up in the morning you'll again have forgotten everything, and you'll again want to start from scratch. Let's just move ahead. We'll ensure we have buffer time at the end of everything. Tomorrow night we'll revise the whole syllabus.'

I knew at the back of my mind that this was going to be far from possible, but Aryan had this glib manner of convincing me that studying Economics was as simple as understanding nursery rhymes. We continued mugging up gory chapters through the night, with intermittent coffee breaks, which were actually meant to make us feel like we had been working the lives out of us. And if there was someone who always had a reason to smile during the nights of examinations, it was the cycle vendor who sold coffee to students burning midnight oil for the sake of a plus three GPA. Owing to us his business did wonders during these days. We went out for a cup exactly every two hours, with the hope of keeping awake and alert for the next two hours, so as to bring out some yield. And during every break, we would hear Sameer and Swapnil arguing over some economics theory we had not read of till then.

Sameer had a passion for Economics, given that he had achieved "Honours" in that subject at graduation college. His knowledge of the subject was remarkable, and he actually spent most of his time sharing his knowledge with us. For about a couple of hours, he actually lectured Aryan, Naina, Vandana and me, trying to teach us fiscal policy and monetary policy. It was the first time I got to see the intellectual mettle that the guy possessed, over and above the upmarket image that he had externally. There were times, in fact, when some of us lost concentration midway, but he continued to teach us with consistent passion.

Our group study turned out to be quite a hit during the exam nights. The lighter moments that we managed to steal in between the endless struggle with the curricula, helped us sail through those times without much agony. The exam nights also played a huge role in shaping this camaraderie among the six of us. Soha, on the contrary, never really became a part of our group, except when she tagged along with Sameer when we went out for a dinner or a movie. None of us minded her occasional presence either, though I knew that the others, like me, didn't hold her in very high regard. All that we cared about was that she was very important to someone who was very important to us.

The single biggest merit of studying in a group, I believed then, is that you get to divide your anxiety with the others. Another merit I thought existed was that the condition of all members of the group would be the same at the end of the day, and hence if I were jacked in the exam, so were the others. Only the discrepancies in our report cards a month later would refute this second major assumption I had made.

At 5 AM, we felt a critical need to get some sleep. My mind could take in no more, and my eyes burned with pain. I felt nauseated after having guzzled some n number of cups of coffee and a packet of Parle-G biscuits which I really did not need. We retired to bed, setting the alarm for 9 AM. *Four hours for completing our respective portions, three hours for explaining our portions to each other, and four hours of buffer for revising the entire syllabus,* was Aryan's "calculated estimate".

We slept till ten-thirty, hunted for breakfast till twelve, and finally settled down again to work at twelve-thirty. We raced with time, and were beaten fair and square. We ate into our buffer time that we had kept for "revising" the course. Post midnight, both of us thought we had achieved something close to the completion of our syllabus, but we had no time or energy left to go through the same stuff once again.

'I can't seem to remember a thing,' I said in dismay.

'Don't worry,' Aryan assured, 'once you start writing the first few words, the rest will automatically follow. And anyway the faculty doesn't have time to read the whole answer. We just need to get the first few lines right. We can gas our way through the rest!'

'For God's sake, Aryan, this is not a literature exam,' I said. 'You can't "gas" in Economics. They need accuracy.'

'Trust me bro, I've done it in college too. If you think you can't remember much, just start using flashy statements like "The economy is on a boom", and "Market prices are sensitive". They like statements like those. And wherever possible, draw a figure or a graph with three different coloured pens. I think everything will be just fine.....'

CHAPTER 9

Velocity Tonight

The travel agency office in Vile Parle is one cramped enclosure, with room for barely two visitors to sit at a time. Sameer and I sat in there since ten AM, waiting to meet the manager. The exams had just ended, and we had managed to squeeze out three days thereafter for a short holiday, and were trying to figure out various possible destinations. After a great deal of brainstorming the previous night, we had boiled down to three options: Goa, Mahabaleshwar, and Daman. Price was a big consideration, and we were trying to find the most inexpensive place and the most economical mode of travel. Naina and Vandana had backed out of the plan, and that had actually saved us the fuss of looking for luxurious travel and accommodation arrangements.

After almost an hour of rendezvous with the pesky houseflies in the room, the manager walked in. He was completely round in shape, with a tummy that showed signs of affluence. He wore in his neck a big locket weighing at least a kilo, and his shirt had very gaudy-golden embroidery all over. He chewed *paan,* with a little amount of paste spurting out of his mouth every time he spoke.

'Hello friends, I am The Kamlesh Shah! How can I be helping you?'

'We were looking at certain travel options and we need to decide between Goa, Mahabaleshwar and Daman,' I began. 'So we needed you to give a few suggestions in terms of what are the places worth seeing, the cost of travel, etc.'

'See friends,' *The* Kamlesh Shah said, 'Goa is too hot right now. I suggest that Mahabaleshwar is good idea. Nice weather and very nice food. Also my brother is running his restaurant there, with special Gujarati dishes for cheap rates. You will like it. And for breakfast he also...'

'The food thing can be considered later,' Sameer interrupted him. 'First tell us about the travel facility you provide, as well as the rates.'

'Eight hundred bucks per person-one way,' his voice suddenly became serious and less friendly.

'Eight hundred!' we exclaimed in unison. 'Boss, please tell us the correct rates, we are students. We can't afford that much.'

'Look friends, travel rates that I am telling you are much cheaper than anywhere else you can find in the city. It is actually one thousand bucks but I am already giving you twenty percent discount because I am knowing you are students.'

'Thanks a lot!' I said sarcastically. 'We will come around later if we decide upon something.'

Back in college, we sat with Aryan and Swapnil, giving them all details we could gather. Sameer, in typical boardroom meeting fashion, took out a piece of paper and drew a table.

Options	Hours of travel	Possible modes of travel	Likely constraints
Goa	12	Train, car, bus, hovercraft	Time, heat, higher cost
Mahabaleshwar	3	Bus, car	Comparatively less sight-seeing
Daman	5-6	Bus, train, car	Heat, less liquor

'Let's do a cost-benefit analysis first,' Sameer said, still apparently caught in the examination fever. After a long debate, we decided to freeze our decision on Mahabaleshwar. Just as we were preparing to leave college to get the tickets booked, we saw a big notice flash on the soft board near the entrance:

Attention First Year Full Time MBA Students: SPG Confectioneries Coming on Campus for Summer Placements Tomorrow. Those Interested Must Submit a Hard Copy of Their Biodata in the Placement Office Latest by 4 PM Today.

We looked at one another for a minute, and then without a word, we retreated towards the library, took out our laptops, and began preparing our resumes. 'Damn, this plan was too good to be true,' Aryan said. We all felt deprived of a break that we felt we really deserved. And now we were going to get into this rut of a schedule of companies pouring in every two days to recruit students for their summer internships.

'Well, the plan is not cancelled dude,' Swapnil said in a cool, reassuring tone, 'look at it this way. If we go after our summer placements happen, we will be able to enjoy it better. And it will be a double cause for celebration.' It was hardly a consolation, but for now, we had to live with this hope.

Preparing the resume was no big effort, until we reached the section of "Academic Achievements". While the others had already submitted their copies in the placement office,

Aryan and I were still discussing what to write under that heading.

'I got a "Best disciplined student of the year" award in class 6,' I said, 'do you think I could write that down? Or is it too back in time?'

'Yeah sure, why not,' said Aryan, 'even I can mention my "100% attendance in the year" certificate of class 4. I think they'll be damn impressed!'

We finally did manage to think of a few measly points here and there, which by some stretch of imagination did qualify as academic achievements. Our deficiency there, however, was compensated by the section of "Extra-curricular Activities", in which both of us had a good deal to write. Our interest in music yielded fruit somewhere, after all. We finally submitted our resumes in the nick of time, hoping that companies would also consider the "all-round development" of the candidate rather than merely looking at his academic feats.

The news of the summer process beginning at such short notice had all of us in the doldrums. The MBA course was living up to its reputation of giving its students sleepless nights and days of toil. We had hardly recovered from the examination debacle that the next shell had been hurled too.

'Hey guys, cheer up!' Sameer came running to us excitedly like he had just discovered an eighth wonder. 'Soha just called. She says…'

'Soha calling up must be a reason for you to cheer, Sameer...' I began.

'Cut it out jackass,' he chided, 'she called to inform us that she has five complimentary couple passes for Velocity tonight!'

'What's that?' Swapnil asked coldly.

'It's the coolest disc in Mumbai. The who's who of tinsel town comes there.'

'Well, I guess you can count me out chum! I am really not in the mood tonight. I'd rather stay in college and look up some stuff for the interview tomorrow.' Swapnil said.

'Me too! I think I'd rather catch up tonight on some sleep,' concurred Aryan, 'look at me! I look like a zombie!'

'And what about you?' Sameer looked at me.

'I don't mind coming,' I said, 'but I don't have a partner. Who do I dance with?'

'That's not a problem. You have more than ten hours to look for one. So I'll see you at nine.'

Going to Velocity was a tempting proposition, but randomly asking a girl out for a dance was going to be equally difficult. I was pathetic at it, and I knew I would not be able to pull it off so easily.

'Why don't you ask Vandana?' Aryan suggested.

'I'm not sure if she would want to.'

'You can ask her anyway!' Sameer persisted.

I saw Vandana in the library, reading something with intense concentration.

'Hey, what's up!' I greeted her.

'Hi!'

'How were your exams?'

'They were OK. Let's see, only the results will tell.'

Typical remark by someone who knew he or she had done marvelously well.

'What about you?' she asked.

'Let bygones be bygones.'

Typical remark by someone who knew he or she had screwed up big time.

'But this is insane!' I continued. 'The authorities should be considerate enough to at least give a small break after the exams. This is mental stress at its peak. We had planned a trip to Daman, but it all went down the drain with the news of this summer process coming like a bolt from the blue!'

'I know,' she said, 'it was pretty sudden. They gave us absolutely no time.'

'Sameer did come up with this idea of us going to a disc tonight, though. He has got a few couple passes as well. He has been pestering me since morning to come along.'

'So why don't you go?' she asked, 'It should be fun!'

'Yeah, but I don't have a partner! Basic problem, you see!'

I waited for her to offer to come along.

'There are so many girls in our college who would be ready to go. All you need to do is go and ask one of them!'

Isn't that precisely what I am doing, lady?

'Nah, I don't know any of them that well. I have hardly spoken to most of them. Say, why don't you take my pass and go to the disc? At least it won't go waste!'

Vandana studied me for a moment, and then burst out laughing. 'Alright, Nakul, I'll come with you. What time is it?'

'Ten thirty,' I said, smiling sheepishly.

CHAPTER 10

Who Isn't Manipulative?

'Sameer! Is this my mouthwash lying in your bathroom?' I shouted, banging his bathroom door shut behind me.

'Yeah,' Sameer replied absently, as he dabbed yet another variant of cologne onto his handkerchief, 'I used a bit.' He sniffed heavily into his handkerchief.

'A bit?' I shouted again. 'You've swigged down half of it already, you ass! It's Listerine, after all, not some cola.'

Sameer didn't reply. He continued religiously the exercise of applying cologne on the kerchief, putting it to his nose, and then shaking his head in utter disapproval.

'With the amount of time you're taking to get ready,' I said, 'there looks like more than just dancing on your agenda.'

He smiled, still not looking up at me. Shying away, he said quietly, 'Maybe.'

'Maybe what?' I prodded him.

'Ok listen, this is just between you and me,' he whispered, closing the room's door behind him. 'Soha called some time back and said that her parents are leaving town for the weekend, and that she is not comfortable with the idea of staying alone. So I offered to stay at her place for the night, and she agreed!'

'Well…and?' I prodded him further.

'And…whatever!' he replied, blushing all the more.

I looked at him without saying a word.

'What happened?' Sameer asked. 'You think it's not right?'

'Not so,' I replied, 'just that I hope you know what you are doing. I mean, just because a girl pulls your cheeks or ruffles your hair in public, it does not necessarily mean she loves you.'

'I love her,' Sameer cut in, 'nothing else matters.'

I nodded in acquiescence. That statement was like a final word, and true in its own right. If he loved her, it was indeed nobody's business to advise otherwise.

'Oh, by the way,' he continued, 'look what I've bought for her.' He brandished an exotic pearl necklace.

'Good God!' I exclaimed. 'That must have cost you a bomb!'

'It did, but it's worth it.' He said. 'I plan to give it to her tonight.'

'That's nice,' I said, not sure how nice an idea it really was. 'Are we ready to leave now, if you are finally dressed?'

'Yes, we are, 'he said, 'just two minutes more.'

People who believed that only girls were finicky about choosing their evening dress should have seen Sameer rummaging his wardrobe since seven that evening. His room was in sixes and sevens after he had tossed almost every cloth from his cupboard and flung it to almost every corner of the room, just to find the right match for his corduroys. White was too sober, red was too bright, and black was just too plainly black for him. He had a shirt of each primary colour, and a shirt of each possible permutation and combination of each of those primary colours. And when he finally did select a shirt, it had taken him another hour to shave meticulously, ridding himself of every speck of hair from his face.

'Alright,' he said finally, looking with a satisfied look in the mirror, 'we are off.'

The disc had a huge and wide marble floor, with enough space to accommodate three hundred people. Halogen lights of different colours flashed on my face, and the music played at a deafening volume. A highly enthusiastic disc jockey played a range of Hindi, English pop, Punjabi, Arabic and hip-hop music and bounced constantly at the same place like a yoyo. A myriad variety of the Mumbai junta was present: the happening, the not-so-happening, and the wannabe happening. There were people lounged around in corners, in happy spirits, drinking and smoking away to glory, cuddling with their better halves. On the floor, there were couples dancing the retro-style, groups of teenagers dancing the *Ganapati Visarjan* steps, and many others dancing unclassifiable, bawdy Bollywood item number steps, all to the same song. And in the midst of this motley crowd, there was but a single focal point: Soha Sharma, sitting with Vandana in a far corner on a velvet sofa, with her legs perched on a tripod in front of her. Dressed in an extra short red skirt and a white low-cut top, Soha revealed more than necessary, and had been drawing more attention from the guys than Sameer could tolerate.

'Ooo-la-la!' I said in awe, in spite of myself. 'Your girl is truly...'

'Watch it, OK?' Sameer said, slightly annoyed. 'Watch it.'

'My, someone's ultra possessive!' I laughed. 'Ok, I have my mouth zipped.'

As we strode up towards the two girls, we saw Soha gleefully chatting with a guy, who then slinked away into the crowd before we reached them.

'Who was he?' Sameer demanded authoritatively.

'Jealous, huh?' Soha winked. 'Just another random guy asking for a dance. He was the third tonight, and had you not come, I would have said yes to this one.' She pulled him lightly by the collar and brought him down on the sofa, staring into his eyes with her archetypal seductive glare. With one hand, she began playing with his hair, which if done by anyone else, would have irked him off, given the time he had invested into gelling and combing his hair at the hostel. With the other hand, she slowly began working her fingers around his face and neck. It was almost artistic; an act that seemed to have been perfected with infinite experience. They swept across his skin as lovingly as a painter's brushes would caress his canvas.

'Do you want to stay?' Vandana said, turning to me. She shifted embarrassedly in her seat.

'No, we can leave these two here,' I whispered to her, 'let's dance.'

I was not too sure about Vandana, but I, for one, felt a little awkward because I had not been to a disc before. (That is, if I discount my visit to an anniversary party of my parents' friends when I was eight, where there was this artificial set-up with jazzy lights for entertaining kids. I had danced with a very sweet little girl to the Disco Dandiya kind of numbers of the late 80s.)

'I am sorry, I forgot to tell you that I've got two left feet!' I said as we got on the dance floor. 'Have you been to discs before?' I hoped she'd say she hadn't, especially given that Nainital did not, to the best of my knowledge, have any disc.

'Yeah, I have. A couple of times, with my cousins in Delhi,' she said, looking slightly downwards, trying to tune the rhythm of her feet to the tango.

I tried to put up my best possible jig for some half hour or something, trying to learn from the people around us. But my body demanded more space to sway around, and that was getting increasingly difficult as people were closing in on each other with each new entry on the floor. Every now and then, my hands would inadvertently brush against a girl, and I would be faced with a look of accusation, as though I had felt her up.

Soha and Sameer were now on the floor too, her arms locked behind his neck, his wrapped around her waist. They were stuck together like Siamese twins, and were to remain pretty much that way for the rest of the night. The songs changed from one genre to the other, but Soha maintained a constant motion of dance. She would release her hands from Sameer's neck, shift back a bit. Then she would raise her hands up and swirl them through her hair till her long tresses curled up into a ball. Then she would swing her hips from left to right, four times, turn around and protrude her hips outward, and then gyrate from left to right again. She would then take a rapid turn back and face Sameer again. Then, bringing one foot forward, she would gently lift the edge of her skirt by a few centimeters, and before anyone knew it, would drop it back down, move a step forward, and lock her arms around his neck again. Then the whole sequence would be repeated mechanically. Sameer, on the other hand, was hardly dancing. He was shifting from one foot to the other, at the same place, at the most. Half tipsy already, he had submitted the remaining half of his attention to Soha's luscious moves.

And then, we witnessed what I feared the most. Sameer fetched out of his pocket the pearl necklace, which dazzled in all its splendour in the darkish room. No sooner did he tie the jewel around Soha's neck, than she instinctively leaned forward and kissed him. Then again, and again, and again. And then followed a longer kiss, which was seemingly unending.

Vandana was scandalized. 'Ah, I didn't know anything was cooking!'

'I didn't either,' I said, half-lying.

For the remainder of the time, I found it difficult to dance. My attention was now on the disaster that was manifesting in my friend's life less than five feet away. I had no solid evidence to call it a disaster then, but a strong vibe gave me reason to feel so. Vandana got the hint, and beckoned me to get off the stage.

'I am sorry,' I said, 'I think I don't make a very fine dance partner!'

'Hey no,' she said, 'I was *actually* tired. And though I did not admit it initially, but I've got two left feet myself!' She grinned. 'Care for a midnight snack?'

'Sure.'

Reflecting the typical Mumbai nightlife, the eateries outside the disc played host to a large number of customers even past midnight. We ordered our burgers, and managed to find exactly one table in the centre of the food mall.

'This is outrageous!' I said, still unable to get over the romance flourishing inside.

'Why? Aren't you happy for Sameer?' Vandana asked, picking slices of tomatoes escaping her burger. 'Or was he competition for you?' She asked me with a grin.

'You got to be kidding,' I scorned, 'I would not, for the life of me, fall for someone like Soha. And I wish he would not either.'

'Why?' She asked, almost examining me curiously.

'I just think the girl is...manipulative.'

'Who isn't?' Vandana shot back instantly. 'Who isn't manipulative?'

'I didn't get you. You mean, am I manipulative too?' I asked, taking guard for my image.

'We all are, I am afraid. You, I, all of us. Aren't we?'

'I don't think I am. I don't think you are. I don't think any of my close friends are, for that matter.'

She looked me in the eye for a few seconds, as though trying to make an assessment of my thoughts. 'You really are very possessive about your friends, aren't you?'

'Yeah, I guess I am. Why?'

'I am, too, unfortunately,' she mused.

'Unfortunately?'

'Yeah. I have had past experiences that have told me that friends are good as long as you don't pin any expectations against them. But as a friend gets close, expectations are conceived. And the higher the expectations get, the more you start feeling that your expectations are not met. One thing leads to the other, and you end up in a cesspool of emotional crisis.'

'You seem to have gone into rough weather in the past,' I said, 'is there something you would like to share?'

'No,' she laughed, 'I am over and above these things. I was just sharing a thought.'

'Well, I agree with you in part,' I said, 'but this is a largely unavoidable menace. I mean, I don't think attachment to someone and expectations from him or her are a planned move.'

'Exactly,' she said, 'which is why, all said and done, I still get close to every new friend I make-like I am now close to you all.'

I smiled, and continued feasting on my burger, letting her words pass. But thereon, I was to be subconsciously reminded of her words time and again.

When we walked back to the disc, we saw Sameer and Soha were already at the exit gate, ready to leave. The kissing had not really stopped; continual displays of affection were still being performed here and there.

'We are beat,' Soha said, smiling from ear to ear. She hung on to Sameer's shoulder constantly with one hand, and kept playing with her necklace with the other.

'We are going to her place for a chat,' Sameer said, evidently stressing on the word *chat*. 'You can also come, if you like.' His last line was extremely low on decibel. We almost had to strain ourselves to hear it. Then, he quickly positioned himself behind Vandana, and stared at me with widened eyes, wagging his head fervently.

I smiled. 'No, thanks. I'll be off. You guys go ahead.'

'Me too,' Vandana was quick to add, 'I will see you guys in college tomorrow.'

The couple did not insist for the second time. Gaily, they trotted across the road, hitched a cab, and were soon out of sight.

For the next couple of months, we saw Soha, with the unexaggerated elegance and charm of a sorceress, draw Sameer steadily into a whirlpool of hopes and fanciful dreams, in return riding on arguably the most fun-filled moments of her life, only at the expense of the emotions of someone who was madly in love with her. Sameer sat extra hours and taught her lessons done in classes that she missed due to party hangovers the previous night. He finished her pending assignments when she could not keep extra hours in college on account of her countless social obligations. He dropped her at her Bandra residence every evening after classes so he could spend an extra hour with her. And of course, there were those frequent dinner treats that kept happening at their regular intervals.

Many weeks after the night at the disc, I had got brazen enough and had asked Sameer what happened that night at Soha's place. 'It was amazing,' he had replied, 'I have never before felt so in love, never before as complete as I felt when I held her in my arms that night in bed.' He went on to add that the fact that Soha was so full of life despite all the worries she bore, made him love her even more. What kind of worries, I asked him.

'Her father has been steadily losing ground in their textile business. They have also been running out of luck in the share market, and their family is practically living on fringes for now. She is wondering how she will afford to buy her laptop for next semester's Market Research classes.'

How will she manage, I asked out of concern.

'I am buying it for her. I have spare money left, thanks to the educational loan I opted for.' He said with pride. He said it with love. A statement right out of the heart. A heart of gold.

If Soha's family was living on fringes, it took little effort to wonder how she afforded the swanky lifestyle that she flaunted. But, besotted by the magic of her doe-like eyes and sugary facade, Sameer's emotions dominated over sanity and logic. Beginning with Naina, each one of us tried our hand at talking him out of the mess that he was getting into. But each time we were greeted with an obstinate, almost indignant opposition from him. That left us with little option but to wait and watch before the curtains would rise over the farce that the temptress showed.

CHAPTER 11

We Need To Strategize

Leaving aside certain landmark events like the system of my laptop crashing, issuing my first book from the library which I never read, and the Mumbai monsoon finally coming to a halt, little significance could be attached to the period between the end of our first trimester exams and our Diwali break. This duration elapsed soon, but the break passed by even sooner. And before we could realize it, we were back in Mumbai for the second round of infliction by the rigour of nine new subjects. The vacation did give us respite from the sedate lectures, the penalties for late submission of huge assignments, and the bland hostel food. But at the same time, it made us miss the lighter moments spent on the campus lawns, our jamming sessions in the hostel corridor, and the crass jokes we cut at Rama's tea stall near the college gate. It made us miss the mock "group discussions" we had on the terrace of our hostel in those starry evenings.

Rigour and tension had an interesting way of greeting us after the leisure time we spent at home. The first message that flashed on the notice board at the entrance was: Kind Attention First Year Students: - Results of the First Trimester Examinations out. Results on Display at 2 pm.

A strange feeling crept into me. My gut began to churn, and my limbs went cold. I was almost certain I had flunked in at least one subject. It was just a matter of three hours before I knew what deep shit I had landed myself into. And it is normally these few hours, before destiny sticks its tongue out to you in mockery, which make life miserable for you. It was, as a matter of fact, not even destiny that I could blame. Whatever I was going to see three hours from then was a consequence of my own laxity. But then, it's always been convenient for most people to blame fate for their state of wretchedness, and I was no exception.

But bad things come in very large packages–larger than one can normally handle. Our professors decided to give us our Diwali bonanza on the first day post vacation even as we were handed mammoth assignments in almost all subjects for the coming week. 'Class, I am giving you four "small" case studies of which you have to do a critical analysis–minimum five hundred words each, by next Monday.' This was the only line I actually made note of in our entire three hour long lecture on Corporate Strategy that morning. The rest of the two hours and fifty nine minutes my mind had wandered away to the spooky visuals of a computerized sheet with my name on it, and a big "F" printed in bold against my name.

At the strike of two, I stood in the administrative office staring at the computer screen in front of me, so as to ensure I got the bad news before anyone else walked in. After a few more agonizing minutes, the screen showed me something that would be hard to believe for days to come.

Roll No: 22

Name: Nakul Kapoor

Result: PASS

I scrolled up and down a number of times and scanned the entire web page repeatedly. I was too overwhelmed to speak. I just walked up to the counter and spoke to the in-charge.

'Can I have my report card, please? Roll number 22.'

By now, the office had got swarmed with two hundred anxious students collecting their report cards, drawing comparisons with each other, and trying to see where they stood in the maddening race. My CGPA read 2.86/4, which I was pretty satisfied with, or rather, I deserved to be content with just that. But that satisfaction lasted only till I was unaware of what grades the people around me had got. Swapnil had topped the batch with 3.83, and most others in my close circuit of friends had notched up a decent 3.30 plus.

For a moment that lasted as long as eternity, I felt alone and desolate, probably for the first time, even as I watched Swapnil, Sameer, Naina and Vandana huddle up in a corner and discuss their merits in loud, excited whispers. A part of me wanted to join them, like I always did. But the other part told me I was a misfit amongst them that day. I prayed I could disappear from the scene and go hide myself in some remote corner. My theory that students studying together in a group would end up with similar performances had just got disproved, and it was not a pleasant feeling. By the time I could leave the office, my grade was known to everyone who mattered and to everyone who did not. I went down, sullen, hoping to find some godforsaken soul who would fall in my league. It would actually not matter much whether or not someone had a lower grade than mine, because mine would still be that screwed up figure of 2.86. But sometimes merely knowing that you are not the lone black sheep of the lot can be a wonderful panacea. After a long, desperate search, I did manage to find a few good men who had kept me company in the sub-three category. But it did look like I was still probably the lowest, and I had set the baseline for the batch. Only about a half hour later, I finally found the remedy I was looking for. The ever dependable Aryan Nair sat aloof, fists locked under the chin in a pose of deep agony, and chewing bubble gum to make himself feel a little relaxed. I went and sat next to him, and tapped him on the knee.

'How much?'

He did not reply.

'C'mon,' I prodded, 'you can tell me. Is it below three? Mine is!'

Yes!! Please tell me yes!!

'2.78!' he said, staring at the blank wall in front of him. 'What's yours?'

Phew!! I may sound like the most selfish swine, but I was glad to hear that. Not that I did not want him to do well, but at that time I needed some comfort, a reassurance that there was at least one of my friends I stood shoulder to shoulder with, which I thankfully got from him.

'2.86,' I said, 'We'll have to make up for this next time.'

'That's stating the obvious,' he replied, 'else we are doomed. All I am wondering is where did we falter?'

*We just need to get the first few lines right. We can gas our way through the rest...Everything will be just fine...*Certain excerpts from the pre-exam days now began to pinch our consciences.

Just then, the biggest nerd of our class walked in with a big sunshine smile. My interactions with him had been, and remained, too few for me to remember his name. I simply associated him with the only *khadi kurta* I ever saw him dressed in.

'Hey guys! Tell me your scores!' *Khadi Kurta* demanded.

'Forget it,' I said dryly, 'it's less than yours for sure.'

'It has to be!' *Khadi Kurta* grinned. 'I topped jointly with Swapnil!'

'Hey that's great news!' Aryan showed a visibly feigned excitement in his voice. 'Congratulations!'

'Thanks,' he smiled. 'But how much did you get?'

Aryan relented to his insistent demand to know our scores, and quietly mumbled something.

'Oh gosh!' *Khadi Kurta* exclaimed. 'Why so less?'

I could swear my frustration and rage urged me to kick the guts out of the fat blob, but some civility held me back. I never understood what ever got people to go ask someone why they brought themselves poor results.

'Just like that–we felt like getting that much,' I said bitterly, 'we consulted some numerologists and they told us these figures were lucky for us this season.'

Khadi Kurta laughed. 'I see, figures that bode prosperity, are they?'

'You got it.'

Now why don't you go take a walk, you pumpkin?

'There's no use being bitter with others,' Aryan said when *Khadi Kurta* left, 'people will continue talking. So let's plan what we do next.'

'Let's make amends,' I said. 'We need to start afresh. Let's put this behind us right now, right away.'

'We need to strategize, otherwise nothing will work,' he said.

I looked at him, mildly amused. 'I think I've heard that before, haven't I?'

He laughed. 'Hey, I think I am too drained today. Why don't we go to the beach and unwind today? We'll start working systematically from tomorrow.'

I remembered the piece of paper I had stuck in my frame by my bedside. *Start studying tomorrow...*

'Ok, done,' I said, getting up. 'Let's hit the beach!'

We trudged our way to the beach, still disconsolate after our dismal show. The dismay of performing badly did not hit us as badly as the fear of its ramifications (read our fear of being at a disadvantage at the time of our placements).

'Do you think companies consider a student's grades while picking him?' I asked him on the way. 'I guess they would rather want to see his all-round achievements, won't they?'

'I don't even want to know right now,' he said. 'What all-round achievements, by the way?'

'Now, let's not underestimate ourselves, Aryan,' I tried to reason. 'I have won quite a few prizes in debates and quizzes in engineering college. And we can always participate in inter B-school management fests now, and show our worth somewhere!'

Aryan shrugged. 'We can't bank on all that. The bottom-line is that we are in a rut and need to get out of it immediately.'

We sat for a long while, staring idly at the dark waves, which reflected in a way the pall that had descended upon us that day.

'I haven't read a single magazine or journal from the library in these many months,' I spoke after a long lull, 'that's where the problem lies. Extra reading always helps to deliver that extra punch in the exams!'

'To hell with the punch,' Aryan said, 'we have not even read our textbook yet. And we can't possibly do justice to the extra magazines and journals without having read our textbook.'

'We need to do both the things side by side,' I said, unsure of what actually we needed to do.

'Won't it make much more sense if we try and understand the concepts first? Build a base first, and then think of the extra gloss.'

Having said that, we prepared ourselves a one-year plan which was to start the next day. We would read a chapter from the textbook everyday, and then discuss it between us. This would give us three weeks to complete all twenty-one chapters. Following that, we would read all the possible magazines and journals of the library, and a minimum of two business newspapers everyday. We would do all our assignments without copying and pasting from the internet. We would complete all projects and presentations well before the time deadline.

We had barely begun to seriously contemplate our course of action, when we got a message from Swapnil: Hi! My Treat for the Result Tonight. Be there at Alfredo's at 9.

'What say?' Aryan asked me.

'Let's go,' I said, *we will start tomorrow.*

'We have time,' he said, 'let's walk here for a while.'

We walked along the waves, mulling over our future. Suddenly, Aryan stopped, walked closer to the water, and opened his arms to the sea dramatically.

'I love it,' he shouted, 'this is what I love about the city. It never makes me feel alone. It never makes me miss Delhi so much!'

'Stop your drama *yaar,* people are looking at you.'

'Which people?' He turned around and asked.

'All of these,' I said, pointing to the numerous couples thronged near the waters, trying to steal a private moment of passion.

Aryan craned his neck around, examining one of the couples very closely. That couple was the farthest of all, and were sitting on a huge rock lying at a distance on the shore.

'Do you see the guy?' Aryan asked. 'He looks like our senior, Sambhav.'

'Aha,' I responded absently, 'good for him. There are some people out there who have all the luck while we brood over our misfortune!'

'The sadist in me tells me to go and cause a rupture in that passionate moment,' Aryan's sullen expression suddenly changed to a wicked, sadistic grin. 'Let's go and say hello to dear Sambhav!'

'Chuck it, Aryan,' I protested, 'that's not right...'

Aryan ignored my suggestion, and strode fast towards the couple. I tagged along. Just a few yards away from them, Aryan balked suddenly, yielding a highly astounded expression.

'Oh my God!' He squeaked in horror.

'What's the matter?' I asked, bewildered.

'That's...that's Soha!' He pointed at the girl cuddled up with Sambhav.

I strained my eyes to look carefully. Soha it was, indeed. We stood behind a food stall to stay out of their sight, but good enough to get a clear view of the scene.

'That's some energy they've got,' Aryan murmured, 'their kissing has lasted quite long, nay?'

'You bet,' I replied, 'they must need oxygen masks!'

The twosome had now got up from the rock, but the kissing had not stopped. Sambhav dug his hands into the rear pockets of Soha's jeans, and pulled her closer towards him. She did a short jump, and clung her legs around his hips. They came closer, until the two silhouettes united under the dim moonlight. The only thing that was still distinctly visible in the dark was the dazzling necklace Sameer had given her the other night. Sambhav took off her jacket, and with it, mistakenly came undone, that costly necklace. Once resplendent in its beauty, the ornament now lay half-buried in the sand, easily within my sight. The couple was now down on the sand, behind the huge rock. We could see nothing more, except for hearing the occasional chortle and shriek.

I took out my phone and furiously dialed a number.

'Hello, Sameer?' I said gravely. 'We are here at the beach. You are not going to believe what we just saw...'

CHAPTER 12

Mutually Great Friends

Naina had a long list of conditions when it came to deciding a place to eat. I first realized it when I asked her where she would like to be treated for helping me in Financial Management. I had, much to my surprise, passed with a decent B+ in the subject, and now dutifully agreed to fulfill my promise.

'Let's see,' she began, 'I am mildly hungry, but not ravenous. So do you have any place in mind?'

'Sukh Sagar?' I asked.

'No way!' she cried. 'The food's too oily there.'

'Bistro's?' I suggested.

'That's only a kebab corner,' she complained, 'I don't think they serve coffee there, do they? A treat isn't complete without a nice hot cup of coffee!'

'Café Corner?'

'The music is so loud there my head aches!'

That was Naina- a girl who had set conditions and prerequisites for everything. She was firm about what she wanted, and could never settle for half a degree less. She may have been senior by age and qualification, but an absolute child at mind and heart. She sulked when things didn't happen the way she wanted them to happen, but then sprang back to joy with a simple Cappuccino or a soul-stirring Jagjit Singh *ghazal.* She had an unconventional charm and a vivacious personality that could make the guys feel weak in their knees, but ironically she did not realize it. Or at least, she claimed that she never realized it. She could be really nasty and caustic in her manner of talking at times, while at other times she could be one of the most amazing mentor-cum-friends I thought I could ever have.

We finally went to Cuppa Café, where she ordered an Espresso Americano (without sugar), a Manchurian Roll, and a handful of tissues. I watched in astonishment as she picked each tissue one by one and caressingly soaked out all the possible oil from the roll till it was reduced to the look of a dry twig.

'Why the big fuss about the calories?' I asked. 'You are in good shape!'

'I am?' she asked, beaming with sudden joy.

'Of course,' I said, 'even round is a shape!', and burst out laughing.

My laughter was cut short by the sudden stern "I will kick the life out of you" expression on her face.

'Sorry,' I murmured, 'just a bad old joke. But seriously, you actually don't need to bother about it!'

She looked much more relieved. 'Yeah, but if I don't do this,' she said, pointing towards the oil-soaked handful of tissues, 'it could cause a lot of damage. Moreover I hardly engage myself in any physical activity. I am too lazy for that!'

The chilly cheese croissant suddenly lost its flavour. I felt my double chin trouble my conscience again. Alright, so I jogged every morning like a maniac. But my fondness for cheese and chocolates had manifested itself in creating their permanent abodes in and around my face and chin. Besides, I never wiped my food with tissues.

'So, what have you decided about summers?' she asked.

Any remaining desire to eat the chilly cheese croissant was completely eradicated by that question.

'Nothing as of now,' I said, pretending to take it very cool, 'I am not sure yet what sector I want to work with.'

'Nakul, twenty-three students have already been placed,' she said in an alarming tone, 'isn't it high time you decided what you want to do?'

Stop sermonizing! Stop being so correct, at least while I am eating!

'Yeah, I'll start applying soon,' I replied, 'just as soon as I get some good corporate projects on hand. I want to put them down on my CV for some more meat.'

Now if there were to be a book titled **101 excuses to avoid preparing for a summer interview**, this line would have been a winner.

'Cut the crap, Nakul,' she cried, 'this is the lamest possible excuse. You are just plain lazy!'

'I've heard that before,' I said sourly, 'so what do you suggest?'

'I suggest you get serious now! Start applying to the marketing companies. If you don't like the experience in the summers, you will at least know *what not* to go for in your final placements.'

'But you haven't applied anywhere yourself, have you?'

'That's because I want to get into credit ratings. Those firms will be coming much later.'

Her words made perfect sense. Twenty-three students were already placed with their summers and I was still not sure of what I wanted. It was an ominous sign, and that was the first day I actually got down to serious business. I began that night itself, by penning down a list of all companies I would want to apply for, and then drafted a customized CV for each of those companies. Drafting a CV for each company was one thing, and working on and revising each project mentioned therein was another. I felt my lack of diligence of the first eight months get more than compensated by the effort I put in that night onwards.

'Alright, I'll get working now,' I said, 'but can we talk about something else at least while we are eating?'

'Hmm, ok,' she said, and paused for a while. 'How is Sameer taking the news of this Soha and Sambhav episode on the beach?'

'I'm sure he's not taking it too well,' I said, 'though if I were him, I would probably not be so shocked to find out what the girl really was.'

'They don't call love blind for nothing, I guess,' Naina mused, 'but such incidents really put me off. It forces me to foolishly doubt the veracity in the words and actions of every person around me.'

I nodded in acknowledgment, and saw her eyes gradually get moist. She stared pensively at the foot of the table, and for a while, there was no exchange of words. A minute later, a large teardrop escaped her right eye, and began to make its way down along her cheek. As it moved each centimeter downward, my mind raced a step backward, recalling every minor and major interaction I had had with her until that evening, beginning with the day she had tirelessly sat with me to explain a subject to me. And I realized, to my surprise, that I had developed for her a respect and admiration that I felt compelled to place on a plane above just another ordinary friendship. What surprised me more was that, the development of this respect was not a function of time either. I found myself, that day, reiterating Sameer's belief that I had so vehemently opposed on a past occasion.

'I've seen this so often before, some in my own experiences too, that it just sickens me.' Naina continued, dabbing her tears with her palms. 'It's difficult to trust anyone.'

I didn't want to know what experiences she was talking about; it was obvious that she had kept them safely vaulted behind closed doors. All that mattered to me was that large teardrop that I was coming to despise, for the sheer pain it was causing to someone I was now boldly ready to claim to be my best friend, and I owned it up to myself to ensure that she was out of the pits.

'It'll never be difficult for you to trust me,' I said, placing my hand in hers, 'I don't know about anyone else.'

She laughed a little. 'I trust you,' she said, patting me on the shoulder, 'I really do. You are a great friend.'

'It's mutual,' I said, 'it's in fact your greatness that percolates down to me when I am in your company.'

She laughed louder this time. 'You sure are a great flatterer, aren't you?'

I was not flattering her. I meant in complete earnestness every word that I said. But I don't think I could ever articulate to her in clear terms what I meant.

CHATPER 13

Kuch Kar Dikhaayenge

Trimesters came and went, but the innate callousness took its own time to cease. Sub-three grades had become a routine event, and Aryan and I became kind of immune to any kind of shock that would emanate thereby. We, in fact, formed a small club of sub-three graders who actually treated ourselves to mini meals at McDonald's each time our results were out. Together with friends, one can look for the funniest of reasons to celebrate. If nothing else, it helps in relieving you of the feeling that you have fallen short of achieving something significant. In our case, our report cards showed us a different perspective: that each time we were getting closer to becoming full-fledged MBAs.

My single biggest achievement in the first year was my summer placement with a reputed pharmaceutical company in Mumbai. A semi-crumpled shirt and zilch knowledge of the pharmaceutical sector notwithstanding, I had managed to pull this one off, and was pretty satisfied with myself.

'We are pleased to have you for our summer training program,' the marketing head said as I shook hands with him. 'We expect you now to live up to our expectations in terms of your effort, and we in turn promise you a rewarding experience.'

I felt tempted to ask him what exactly their level of expectations was, but for some reason refrained from doing so. 'Thank you Sir, it will be a pleasure to work with you.'

The words "pleasure" and "work" did sound paradoxical to me, but now that I had said something to that effect, I thought it would be wise to pull up my socks in any case. I marched to the library with full gusto and got myself two books issued on pharmaceutical marketing.

'You want both together?' the administrator asked me at the counter.

'Yes, I can, can't I?' I asked.

He looked at me for a moment and then let out a cheesy grin. 'Of course you can! You'll have to return both of them in ten days' time.'

'I know that,' I said, 'I'll be done with both of them in four days.'

He looked at me in mock admiration and then continued. 'Have you read "The Blue Ocean Strategy", by the way?'

'No, I haven't. What about it?'

'You got that book issued before Diwali, in case you do not remember! The return of that book is about 81 days overdue. According to the late fee rule of two rupees per day, you are one hundred and sixty-two rupees in debt.'

I flushed in embarrassment and my mind raced hard back in time, trying to recall when I ever laid my hands on a book by that name. It later transpired that issuing this book was a consequence of the discussion Aryan and I had on the beach the other evening. Aryan had said in his trademark style, *'Kuch kar dikhaayenge!'* (*We will show our worth to the world!*) and that had given me a tremendous boost, and subsequently a sudden urge to get hold of the book. The idea of reading the book was to get some useful ideas for the Corporate Strategy exam in the second trimester, but it had remained just an idea at the end of the day.

The third trimester was a three-month long party interjected off and on with a spate of assignments. But these submissions and exams did not seem to affect us much any longer in terms of the mental pressure. Maybe we had got used to the whole thing. Maybe the company of good friends served as an energizer that pulled us out of the jaws of frustration each time we were landed in piles of work.

Partying, bantering around on campus, and exploring parts of the city had become the order of the day. Be it walking down the road to the *burji pav* stall for a midnight snack, be it the missed calls we gave our friends in the classroom whenever we caught them sleeping, or taking light digs at our professors during recess hours in the café, each moment became a phenomenon that etched itself in our Dear Diary pages.

Friends became a necessity, an addiction which we found indispensable. Swapnil and Sameer were our regular saviours during the exams. Swapnil's perfection in imbibing and recapitulating every word and every syllable discussed by the faculty in the classroom, combined with Sameer's insatiable quest to devour all the management journals and e-manuals under the sun, made things very convenient for library-phobic people like Aryan and me to gather all daily scoops that we could use.

Sameer never mentioned Soha again after the beach episode, and we also found it wiser not to prod him with questions on that subject. We were vaguely aware of one more time they had met after the incident, when Soha had tried to play around with the story, giving some hogwash that Sambhav had played angel to her during her past phase of distress, and that she was just being nice to him in return. She accused Aryan and me of having blown the story out of real proportions. But this time, wisdom outdid influenced emotions, and Sameer jilted her that very day. Following that incident, however, Sameer became a changed person. He tended to keep a little aloof. Whether it was because he had developed a general distrust towards everyone around, or whether it was a comeuppance he was serving upon himself for having fallen for a girl who changed her loyalties as per her need of the hour, about as regularly as she got her hair bleached; we didn't know.

Soha had, for her part, already begun to pay for her deeds. By the end of the first year, her tendencies had come to be understood and despised by one and all, and the number of people who had come to despise her as compared to the guys who drooled over her in the beginning looked like two distinct points on opposite sides of the number line, equal in magnitude and opposite in sign. Perhaps one always must pay a heavy price for being opportunistic at the end of the day. The beauty quotient was now out, and frustration and desolation were written all over. Ordinarily, my heart would be compelled to go out to her, because I do know the angst of feeling lonely in a crowd. The "avoid the jerk" vibe that one can get from people around can be a killer. If only the human mind had the capacity of getting premonitions of such situations arising when they behaved like they did, friendship, goodwill and relationships would be much easier to sustain. I felt a disdain when girls like these reiterated my theory of the "girlie girl" and the "bitchy girl". I wanted my theory to be proved wrong somehow.

Thankfully, Naina and Vandana pioneered a digression from this theory of mine. They were the closest to the kind of girls I would feel comfortable with. They weren't the girlie types who carried mascara and a pocket mirror with them all the time, and they never expected guys around them to tell them that they wore pretty tops. Maybe they knew for themselves that they were cute and had a fabulous wardrobe. Whatever the reason was, they spared us the girlie element, and I admired that. They were not even bitchy, because they were free of all malaise, and that was the least I could vouch for if I were to write them a testimonial.

Vandana always made it a point to go and ask every single friend of hers sitting in every single corner of the campus if they would like to come along with her for dinner. Such was Vandana, who knew how to apportion her time for everyone who mattered to her. One could hardly ever complain about any inadequacy in the concern she showed for her friends. A night before our Corporate Finance exam when she sat explaining concepts to Aryan and me, spoke volumes of her dedication. *You will not goddamn yawn or say that you are hungry until you have solved this one on your own,* she had admonished us with a tone of authority for the first time then. The admonishment was well accepted, and that night was one of those rare nights when Aryan and I did not yawn one more time till we were in the library under her watchful eyes.

Naina may have been moderately bitchy, but not by the definition of "bitchy" I stated in my theory, as the intent here was never any kind of mudslinging. Her bitching was rather a form of cribbing, a habit which she could not give up for nuts. She cribbed when her food was too oily, she cribbed if we had to walk more than fifty yards in the heat, she cribbed if she did not get the window seat in all local trains, and she heavily cursed and swore at cars plying on the road if they ended up splashing a drop or two of muddy water on her newly purchased denim. But none of us complained, because she was The Sweetheart of the gang. Besides the fact that our common love for coffee and croissants got us together to explore all the coffee shops and bakery kiosks in the city, she made a great friend, despite the "generation gap" between us, as I often remarked in jest.

Swapnil was one friend I had almost begun to idolize. His sense of timing and planning for every single activity of his day would be the perfect live case study on what an ideal student should be. Dedication was his second name, be it in the hours he sat in a corner of the college talking on the phone to his girlfriend, or in the resolve to chew up every single point in the syllabi of our subjects, or in the sincerity he showed when anyone needed him for a mentoring session.

Aryan and I still made daily time tables. He still kept convincing me that *hum kuch kar dikhaayenge*, and probably this fake assurance kept our guts strong and going all the time. Being with him I learnt that laughing off difficulties was an art. *However bad a situation might be, remember that it could get worse;* we used to tell each other. *So live life king size!*

The network was formed. We had found amongst us the perfect group of friends, which we believed was our biggest strength and our strongest motivator. Before we knew it, a year had passed, and we had to begin working on our summer projects. Vandana and Aryan had their postings in Delhi, while the rest of us remained in Mumbai. But thanks to the "yahoo group" we had created, we remained wired all the time.

CHAPTER 14

No Numbers, No Fun!

Dilip Desai, or DD as I called him, was the only other guy from my college who interned with VRF Pharma. We did not get off to what we could call the most auspicious start to our summer training. Our otherwise ever-reliable BEST bus broke down minutes after it left the first stop from Vile Parle. My watch showed eight forty-five, which meant that we were going to be late for office on the very first day, which in turn meant a severe pounding from the boss.

'What do we do now?' I asked. 'Go to the next stop?'

'Of course not,' DD said, 'the traffic here is a killer on the road. We'd rather take the train from Santa Cruz to Churchgate. Let's move it, now.'

I stalked for a moment as I recalled the first, and only time before that, when I had boarded a South Bombay-bound local in the evening after the induction ceremony. The experience of that travel was not even mildly luxurious, and I had kept myself away from those trains thereon, for the remaining part of the year, until this day.

'What's the other alternative?' I asked.

'Reach office at lunch time!' DD replied sarcastically.

That would not have been a very bad option weighing it against the ordeal I would have to face, standing in a jam-packed local for over forty minutes, on a sweltering May morning. But given the fact that the man we were to meet in the office was going to be our boss we would deal with for the next eight weeks, I gave in to the wiser decision of taking the tougher but quicker alternative to get to our destination.

As we stood at the Santa Cruz platform, we cast intermittent nervous glances at our watches.

'We've had it today,' DD said. 'We won't reach before 10.'

I pictured us entering a long hall with a score of other trainees seated around a table. At the centre would be seated three forty-something grumpy executives, fuming at us, ready to hurl an array of unsolicited comments on our lack of discipline and punctuality.

'Ours is a highly professional organization that respects time. We would expect you to appreciate the same and learn to be a little more punctual than that,' they would say. I thought on our way to office of all possible explanations I could give them so as to minimize the chances of their taking our case.

The train's screech at the platform shook me off my imagination. This time, I was an experienced guy trying to board the train. I leapt ahead, pushed around with all might before I managed to set foot inside. The task was much easier for DD, as he managed to weasel his skinny body through the crowd and conveniently slink inside. For the next forty minutes, I stood still inside the packed compartment, except for the shoving in and shoving out that happened as the train halted at each subsequent station. Beads of sweat dropped from the temples of co-passengers onto my shirt and hands. Dour scents of their warm breaths blew right into my face as they spoke, and I had no option but to stand still and bear it all. What I did notice, though, was a remarkable transition in my attitude from the last time I had boarded a local. While these sores had vexed me par tolerance the previous time, this time I felt much more immune to them. And over the subsequent eight weeks, I found myself board locals more often. Gradually, I developed a fondness towards the train rides, and a time finally came when I found the train rides to be one of the most memorable things I found in Mumbai.

It was nearly ten thirty when we finally reached the VRF Pharma office. The corporate estate that housed it was a sprawling complex, adorned with lush green lawns and trees of myriad variety on either side. The benches and fountains under the shade of those trees provided a perfect zone to chill out in the scorching heat. I only did wonder, though, as to why and for whom such arrangements had been made. Because the employees of all the offices in that estate never had any time to look that side, leave aside the possibility of sitting on the benches and feeling the pleasantly cool droplets of water from the fountains spray on their faces. They came to their offices exactly at nine every morning, and always made a straight dash for their cubicles. They would step out occasionally for a smoke after lunch, for something like no more than ten minutes. And they would rather spend those ten minutes standing right outside their office, discussing amongst themselves the stock market behaviour of the day, their pending wok for the month, or in a much relatively lighter moment they would probably be discussing the content of a private email they chanced upon in their boss's inbox. At close of the day, they would be too tired to even contemplate sitting on the benches. They headed straight for the station to catch the evening local back home. The benches remained unused and the water of the fountains unfelt, and it was left to DD and me, as we found later, to find the time to sit there more often than we thought would ever be possible.

We walked up to the HR department on the second floor. Most cubicles on that floor were empty at that time, and we were just about to conclude that there must be a boardroom meeting going on, when we heard some loud guffaws coming from the end of the room. We walked down to see about half a dozen HR executives flocked around the Nescafe vending machine, taking their first break of the day. They were taking a dig at a plump female executive, teasing her about the extra stuff that she had gained after returning from her honeymoon.

'Excuse me,' I said loudly a couple of times before I could get ourselves noticed, 'we'd like to meet Mr. Yash Mehta, the recruitment in-charge.'

'You'll find him in cabin number 12, right at the opposite corner,' one of them said, 'you must be summer trainees, right?'

'That's right, Sir,' DD said. 'We are late because our bus broke down on the way.'

'That's ok,' he replied coolly, 'go right ahead. Yash also walked in just half an hour ago.'

The door of cabin 12 was half-open. We gave a light knock and then peeped in.

'May we come in, Sir?'

Yash Mehta had his eyes dug into his laptop, and was trying to follow something with intense concentration.

'Come right in and take a seat,' he said without looking up at us, 'give me two minutes, though.'

We walked up to his table and stood there for a minute. I felt compelled to take a peek and see what was keeping him that engrossed. I was highly amused when I saw that he was busy playing Mario Brothers on his laptop, and the poor guy did not seem to be able to get his Mario past world 1-3. *If this is what HR managers do all the time, I am not going to think twice before I decide my major specialization,* I said to myself.

'Sir, use Ctrl+Alt together,' I said, clearing my throat, 'it'll give your Mario extra speed while running. Otherwise he'll keep falling off the cliff.'

He suddenly looked up, embarrassed, and immediately hit the Esc button to quit the game, and sat up straight.

'Yeah, good morning,' he said, 'how may I help you?'

'Sir, I am Dilip Desai, and this is my colleague Nakul Kapoor,' DD began, 'we are summer trainees from…'

'O yes!' he exclaimed. 'I've been waiting for you.'

'We are extremely sorry, Sir,' I mumbled, 'we…'

'Don't bother, it's absolutely alright,' he winked, 'do you know what's the best thing about our organization? We are extremely flexible and tolerant in these respects. As long as you deliver results, we will never question you as to what time you enter office, and how long you sit in office!'

I almost jumped in excitement on hearing that. It's not that I wasn't sincere about my project; in fact, this was the first time I had willed myself to try and gain as much value in terms of work experience as I could. But a mandatory requirement to reach my office everyday at Nariman Point at nine in the morning would mean getting up at my Vile Parle residence at six everyday, and that was not exactly a very thrilling proposition.

'I am redirecting you to your guide, Mr. Avinash Jalan, Group Product Manager, Cardiac Division. He'll tell you more about your project.'

Avinash Jalan was a typical executive who had risen through a considerable number of ranks in the organization, but was still not sure what he was doing there and whether he wanted to do it or not. Everyday we met him, he looked up at us with the most pitiful expression, like we had just loaded him with the burden of the Andes. The fact that timesjobs.com was always one of the sites that showed on his computer screen could by no means be a coincidence. The first opportunity that gave him bigger moolah and better satisfaction would prompt him to quit his job, and he was to confide in us as much a few weeks later.

'Your project deals with the newly introduced concept of sales force automation in our organization,' Jalan began, 'wherein you are required to study its effectiveness and suggest measures from marketers' perspectives to increase bottom-line growth in our Cardiac Division for prescription drugs.'

DD and I looked at each other, partly confused, partly pepped up for some action, even as Jalan paused to get himself a sip of water. 'Does this sound good to you?' he asked after a while.

'So how do we begin, Sir?' we asked.

'Start by reading up some literature and e-manuals on our Sales Force Automation concept. You'll find plenty of it in the library downstairs.' He looked at his watch. 'But I guess you can now start after lunch.'

The lunches at VRF Pharma were the best things to happen to us for those two months. Unlike the highly predictable menu of *alu gobi, bhindi* and *dal fry* in our hostel, this canteen had a different cuisine everyday. And for foodies like me, overstuffing my plate always served as an undesired sedative in the afternoon sessions of office. The most notable thing about the office was that all employees consumed the entire ninety minute duration allotted for the lunch break. And if that were not enough, shortly after the lunch break ended at two, fifty percent of them would be found absent again from their seats by half past two, only to be found near the coffee vending machine, chatting away to glory again.

The library had books on all topics under the sun, ranging from literature on the pharmaceutical industry to gossip magazines of the glitterati. The comfy velvet sofas were a massive temptation to stretch and put myself to sleep, especially after a good lunch, so in the initial days I made a conscious effort to avoid the sofas and take an upright position on the straight chairs and the table. On the first day, we meticulously read and took down notes of whatever we found significant in the SFA manuals. We compared the pre and post SFA implementation sales figures in the Cardiac Division, and made note of the difference the SFA had made in the growth of sales.

By around five that evening, we had prepared a primary draft of our project objective, and a proposal of the methodology we would follow during course of the project. We went up to Jalan's cabin to get his approval, but he wasn't in his seat.

'This is his fourth break since morning that I am seeing him take,' DD hissed.

'Ssh,' I cautioned, 'there are eagles in the air. Don't get us in trouble. And in any case, we should be happy; this indicates we can also take as many breaks as we want to!'

'No boss,' DD protested, 'I, for one, have not come here for a picnic. I have come here to do something worthwhile, and we had better get some good attention and guidance here.'

This was the basic problem working with overly sincere people! They would contradict you just when you would begin to hope there was room for some fun in the midst of work.

Jalan returned after a good twenty minutes. We showed him our proposals and asked for his go-ahead. He read them, and said after a while. 'Yeah, it looks good. Come down tomorrow, and we shall decide how to begin.'

I went back to college that evening after a reasonably satisfactory start. The campus bore an extremely deserted look, with most of our colleagues having got their internship outside Mumbai. I sat in a rather vacant library, and felt a little weird, because I had so far always seen it abuzz with activity twenty-four hours a day. The wi-fi worked that day at supersonic speed, because the internet traffic was almost zero. I whiled away my time by downloading some of my favourite music from the net, even as I waited for Swapnil, Naina and Sameer to return from office.

During those two months, the presence of one or all of these three friends more than made up for the emptiness that engulfed us otherwise. Of course, the circuit was never complete without Aryan and Vandana, but we continued to remain in touch through MSN Messenger, a resource that I fully exploited in the computer lab of my office. Sameer and Aryan found little time online, though, because of their field jobs with their respective FMCG companies. While Sameer always longed for some good experience with a sales and marketing project for his summers, I wondered how someone like Aryan managed to sustain himself even as he worked the life out of himself in the heat of the Delhi market, trying to sell cola cans and potato chips across all retail outlets in the city. Naina and Vandana had relatively sedentary jobs, which allowed them to engage themselves in their daily GDO, or Girls' Discussion Only, as they called it. I often wondered as to what would be the contents of such intense discussions that stretched over almost every afternoon over the chat window. And more surprisingly, both of them always claimed to have *"too much work yaar"* everyday.

Most of my first week at office was spent in the library, although we were done with reading all related manuals at least twice. But Avinash Jalan was purportedly busy for a few days, and hence any progress in our work was kept in abeyance for the first week or so. I tried making constructive use of the spare time that we had by doing what I had not done for almost the whole of first year in college-I read as many business magazines as I could, trying to gain some value during the aestivation period. I also browsed websites and portals related to the subjects of marketing and branding. If nothing more, they gave me a sense of satisfaction of doing something worthwhile after all, that in part at least, justified my purpose of joining an MBA program.

Occasionally after lunch, DD and I would step out of office, and sit on the benches by the side of the fountain. Each time our objective of going there would be to get some peace of mind and try and figure out ways of moving on with our project ourselves. But the perfect setting of the place always managed to distract us, and we always ended up either idly sitting and staring at the thin streams of water dance around the fountain, or picking little pebbles around us and competing as to who could throw them farther.

As time ticked from seconds to minutes to days to a fortnight, however, our anxiety got the better of us. Two weeks into the training program, the value added to our training was at level zero. There was nobody, for quite some time, to tell us what exactly we were expected to do out there. Much that idleness suited my tastes perfectly, this situation meant that the pressure of achieving the humongous project objectives was likely to mount upon us in the last couple of weeks, and that would be a highly unwelcome situation. Our patience finally gave way at the end of the second week, and we decided that we desperately needed some action.

'Please give us some work!' we demanded.

'Ok, what would you like to do?' Jalan asked dreamily, like Rip Van Winkle had just woken up from some long dream and had decided to oblige us.

'We wouldn't know Sir,' DD said, visibly irritated now, 'we were waiting for you to tell us something as to how we must start!'

'Uh-huh,' Jalan pondered, 'I guess you'll have to wait till tomorrow. My boss has asked me to...'

'Sir, please,' we said in dismay, 'we have just six more weeks to go. It'll get increasingly difficult for us to wrap up our work in time.'

'Ok,' Jalan said after some deliberation, 'would you like to go on field and see how things work?'

Now is this a yes/no option game we are playing?

'If it is of relevance to the project,' I said, 'then yes, we'd like to go right away.'

Whether or not the exercise was going to be of relevance to the project objectives was not important. What was important was that it gave us a chance to finally get out of the aestivation mode, and it gave Jalan a chance to get us off his back for at least some time.

'Right then,' Jalan said, 'you can start your field work from tomorrow. I'll book you with a different medical representative for each day. You can go along with them for the week. Watch them closely and report to us your observations. This should help you understand how the SFA really functions in the pharmaceutical market.'

'Alright,' I said, 'and what about the other part of the project? I mean, the marketing initiatives we need to suggest to increase the bottom line...I mean, we are absolutely clueless right now...'

Jalan laughed. 'Don't worry, that will happen after your field visit. I am clueless too. If it were so easy, we would probably not have recruited both of you to help us out!'

One week and a visit to all the clinics of all the suburbs of the city later, we were half a degree less confused and clueless than before. We did get a fair idea about the sales functioning, and the effectiveness of the SFA technique therein. But the second part of the project, which was to draw inferences from these observations and suggest measures to increase bottom-line remained a big ask. The fact that we were novices in the pharmaceutical industry would be a lame excuse to justify our getting stuck midway in course of the project. However, inadequate guidance and support from the top was definitely a very discouraging situation. Each appointment that we sought with Jalan to get some inputs was, more often than not, successfully put into indefinite postponement. Then there were documents that we could use for our reference to gather the required data, but in accordance with the company's security policy, we could not gain access to many of them, as we were not regular employees in the organization. That left us with the sole option of using search engines on the internet, looking for white papers and case studies that could possibly give some guidelines to build on the measures that we were expected to suggest. But a gut feeling told me that this exercise of copying and pasting existent data from external sources was not quite likely to get us a pat on the back from the senior management.

Then one day, some time into the fourth week, my worst fears came true. DD was down with fever and had not come to office. I sat at my cubicle, doing my daily routine of grappling with Google's secondary data sources, when Jalan walked into my cubicle. His reddened face was contoured with multiple frowns that showed signs of severe tension. His jaw dropped low, and beads of sweat formed on his forehead. Surely, there was something more than the summer heat that had been bothering him.

'What's the status of your work, Nakul?' Jalan asked frantically. 'Have you come up with something concrete?'

I had no idea as to what "something concrete" would be for him. 'Not much yet,' I said. 'But I have begun to prepare something. Why, is there some emergency?'

'Oh yes,' he said, his voice shaking. 'Mat called this morning. He is flying down from Singapore on Friday, and he wants to see the status on this project. It is on top of the agenda of his visit.'

Mat, or Vimal Mathur, was Jalan's boss, the marketing head for the diabetic division across the Asia Pacific region, and a terror for most people who worked under him. Reportedly, Jalan had borne the brunt of his terror one time too many, and Mat had apparently never felt too happy while doing Jalan's quarterly appraisal. Unfortunately for Jalan, and indirectly even for DD and me, overseeing our project progress was one of his performance tasks set for him for the coming quarter.

'I'm afraid there isn't much to show him yet,' I said quietly, 'except this much.'

I handed Jalan a bunch of loose papers, containing largely unstructured chunks of information I had gathered from the internet.

'What the hell is this?' Jalan shouted angrily, his expressions of tension suddenly transforming into wrath. 'You expect me to show this nonsense to Mat?'

His decibel levels were high enough to grab the attention of at least twenty people sitting in the room. I seethed with rage on hearing his barrage that went on for the next couple of minutes. For the first three weeks, he found no time or need to attend to us and monitor our progress, leave alone giving us some critical leads that we expected him to provide us in the initial days. I tried to calm him down, negotiating with him for an extended deadline, but his fear of Mat deafened him against my pleas.

'I should have known not to expect much from you!' he scowled, flinging my papers back on me. 'You students think the brand name of a reputed institute can help you get away with anything. But now I have news for you. I am going to give you a tough time- a very tough time. You had better shape up or else be prepared!'

As he walked away, I felt the earth cave in beside me. All employees in that room had discontinued their work, and looked at me with sympathetic eyes. They murmured amongst themselves, but their voices got diffused around the humiliation that filled my senses.

I waited that entire day for evening, so that I could let myself out of there. At the strike of five, I walked out, and headed for the seaside walkway at Haji Ali. The hour that I walked there would count as one of the darkest and loneliest hours of my two years- until I finally decided to call Naina.

'Hi!' Naina said in her trademark cheerful voice as she picked up the phone. 'What's up, boy?'

'Nothing's up,' I said in a flat tone, 'it's the pits!'

'Hey, you sound awful. What's wrong?'

'Just about everything, I'd say,' I said. 'You can say I was shown my place today.'

'Listen, I'll come and meet you after office,' she said after some time, 'where are you?'

'Haji Ali sea side.'

'Haji Ali sea side!' she exclaimed. 'What are you doing there?'

'Feeding pigeons!' I replied coldly

She sighed. 'Just be cool, I'll be there.'

I sat by the Haji Ali snack centre, in a seemingly endless wait as I fought a lone battle against the apparition of Jalan's wrath I faced that morning. The strong aroma of strawberry yoghurt being cooked in the kitchen filled the air, antagonizing the bitterness for Jalan that curdled within me.

'Firstly, you are no God,' Naina said when she met me a while later, 'so don't sulk if you have faltered. It is only human to err. And again, Jalan is no God either. It is also only human to get psyched out if...'

'Jalan is no human,' I shouted excitedly, 'he is a...'

'Ok, whatever he is,' she raised her hand to stop me, 'it should not really matter to you. You need to understand what you got to do now.'

'That's what I can't understand, Naina,' I said dejectedly, 'I just can't. For the first time, I mean it, yes, for the first time, I was willing to put in my best. But there was no support. And to top it, he had the gall to make a scene in front of everyone.'

Silence filled the air between us once again, as Naina hunted for words. We stared for a while at the dark sea, before she spoke again. 'What others speak is something that is not under your control. What *is* under your control is to decide what you must pay heed to and what you must discard.'

'Then here's my decision, I discard Jalan's invectives, because they are not justified.' I said. 'I, in fact, discard him as my boss because he doesn't deserve that authority. He has no standing of his own and he tries to be funny with me.'

'Alright, alright,' she said, patting me on the shoulder in a comforting gesture, 'you can discard him if you please. But you must also pay heed to a lesson that you can learn from this experience.'

'What's that?'

'I'll tell you if you are willing to listen calmly.'

'I'll try.'

'What you must pay heed to is the fact that you need to evolve,' she said softly, 'because all said and done, there is a tinge of bitter truth that lies in the entire incident. We can get away with being casual in our approach to college assignments and exams, but the corporate culture is different. They are ruthless and unsparing, and don't give in to any justifications, however true they may be, as they were in your case. I understand we are all raw in our evolution right now, and it's easy for me to comment on your situation as an external viewer. But what I am talking about actually applies to all of us.'

'So what do you suggest?' I asked.

'I suggest that you don't let this incident take a toll on you. If you feel you have done what you could do best, ignore this day like any other insignificant moment that may have occurred in your life. Over and above that, for your own sake, try and ensure you find out how you can improve over yourself each day - not in terms of this summer assignment, but from a long term point of view.'

That evening, I surrendered myself involuntarily to the manacles of this friendship. That evening, I felt grateful to the serendipitous moment that made me first meet her. That evening, I defined this to be the perfect friendship there could ever be. And that evening, I made a very big mistake. I benchmarked all her actions in the future against the definition of this perfect friendship, and against all the parameters that lay within that definition. And the mistake that I made here was that those parameters remained known only to me, and I could never let them be known to her.

The remaining five weeks of summers did not drag. I would rather conveniently call them a summer vacation. I reciprocated with full warmth to my company by assuming the role of a guest appearance in the office, with an average frequency of one visit per week. I spent the rest of the days in the comfort of my air-conditioned library in college, where I had the freedom to work as long as I wished to and make merry whenever I wanted to. It's not like I didn't work, in fact I can safely say that I worked reasonably hard on my project. But I just stopped worrying as to where I was headed. I reconciled myself to understanding that my work would not be taken note of until my final presentation at the end of the internship, where the big bosses would finally be kind enough as to tell me where I went wrong. *I'll learn from my mistakes,* I said to myself. Naina was right after all- if nothing else, summer training does at least tell you what **not** to do in the future.

Every evening of the summer vacation was a party of sorts, especially once the junior batch came in. There were a handful of us seniors who sat in college every evening to welcome them with novel ragging sessions. Sameer and I, in fact, had been working on this "project" for quite long. From the day the first list of the junior entrants had been put up, we had begun shortlisting by name and age criteria the girls we would rag individually. The day finally came when a fresh lot of nervous yet enthusiastic souls made their way into this world of MBA. Sameer and I took a half-day-off from work (not to mention that most of my days were offs anyway) to make a perusal of the batch. To our dismay, half of the batch looked older than us, and that included the girls. Unperturbed by that, however, we did rag them that evening, and did so for many more evenings to come. It was the best pastime we had after the day's toil and frustration.

I began preparing my presentation and project report in the final week of my internship, trying to cover up any inadequacy by adding jazz and jargon of the world into one report. I felt proud of myself. It often made me wonder if I would have made a better career as a journalist or a poet. Unfortunately, however, the jazz and jargon did not permeate through the wise mind of my marketing vice-president who called me for the presentation.

'I have only ten minutes,' was his first line, 'so let's get down straight to business. Please show me your findings and recommendations.'

That was the first mistake I committed. Our classroom habit of gassing our way through by means of needless introductions to our presentations and redundant statistics which were anyway available on ORG Marg, had to be dispensed with here. I reacted promptly by cutting as much slack as possible from my meat and began with a disclaimer:

'Sir, the correlation analysis that I have drawn through last month's sales in Mumbai is an estimate and may not be accurate, because I could not get all the requisite data from the sales department. However, from whatever data I collected...'

'What do you mean by "could not get all the requisite data"?' he snapped in between. 'It was your prerogative to extract the maximum possible from them, right? Who stopped you?'

'Right, Sir,' I nodded quietly.

Second mistake: Never tell an organization that its resources are inadequate. It's a futile complaint and causes offence.

'In view of the enormous customer base that we have, I recommend that we segregate our customers on the basis of the proportion they contribute to our revenue. For that purpose I recommend putting into practice a customer lifetime value model, which will help us decide which doctors we need to concentrate on more for our sales pitches and promotional activities...We can start VRF club memberships or the likes, wherein we can include the top slab doctors as privileged customers of the club...we can invite physicians to deliver lectures at medical forums wherein they can in turn promote our drugs to younger doctors...they will act as key opinion leaders.....offering customer delight is what will go a long way in maintaining a healthy relationship with the doctors...'

"Customer Delight"! Bah! I found it hard to believe my own words and the ease with which I went on ranting virtually the entire textbook of Kotler in front of my VP. I went on breathlessly for a whole ten minutes and finally turned to look

at him. He wore a semi-disgruntled look, but was still smiling. *Corporate norms or sarcasm,* I wondered.

'Hmm, do I have to send a feedback or something like a grade to your institute?' Mr. VP asked.

His question left me reeling. I already knew what I was in for.

'Yes...Sir!' I said quietly. 'But I am ready to take all feedback positively.'

'I am happy to hear that,' he said, 'please take a seat.'

I took a seat in front of him, and closed my eyes, mentally preparing myself to face the tirade.

'Do you know the single biggest thing that was absent from your presentation?' he asked me.

'What?'

'Addressing your project objective!' he said. 'If you recall, you had been asked to suggest measures to increase bottom-line growth. Where is all that?'

It evaporated with the gas, Sir!

I fumbled for words, but he interrupted me and continued. 'Allow me to give you a piece of advice. The terminology that you used in your presentation was good, but it looks good only in the textbook. In the real corporate world, we go only by numbers. Remember - no numbers, no fun! Any and every decision we take related to any aspect of our business is backed by solid numerical data and mathematical proof.'

Reality check to the core!

'It's alright,' he went on, 'I understand it's difficult to absorb everything especially when you are right out of the classroom. But I guess this served as a good learning platform, didn't it?'

'It sure did, Sir,' I said.

'As for the recommendations you have mentioned,' he said, 'they are nice and are worth giving a thought. I only wish there were some more stuff from your side that could help consolidate whatever you said.'

As I took leave of him, I felt tempted to turn back and ask him what feedback he intended to write for me. But some wisdom dawned upon me at the last moment and I decided against it.

My training was over and done with. I walked out of the corporate estate that afternoon with a freer mind, but a firmer resolve. Having understood now what **not** to do thereon, I had a positive sense of direction and had attained a fair idea of what all needed to be done. I put these ideas in abeyance however, then, and made merry with friends for the last week of our "vacation". By June end, we had the menus of all major restaurants in town at the tip of our tongues, we had watched every single movie that hit the screens during that time, we had watched every single play that opened at Prithvi theatre, and we partied in discs and pubs like there were no tomorrow. We were, in fact, a wee bit upset when the vacation ended and the second year classes resumed. But Aryan's vivacity and Vandana's contagiously effervescent smile pretty well nullified the same. We were happy that we were together again. The party was on...

CHAPTER 15

Dimple Doll

July 5, 2005. 9 A.M:

'Nakul, do you know which class this is?'Vandana asked as she entered the classroom on day 1 of the second year.

'Division A, is that right?'

'Yes, for majors in marketing, and minors in Finance!'

'Right, that's what brings me here too!'

'What?' she asked with eyes wide open in astonishment. 'You are minoring in Finance? Whatever prompted you to do something like that?'

'Well, well,' Aryan butted in, 'our boy has just decided to get a little adventurous here!'

'Very funny!' I said. 'I chose it by method of elimination. The other options were either too boring or too digressive from my career path.'

'Career path!' Aryan exclaimed. 'So you finally found it, huh?'

'Yeah, you could say that,' I said, 'you tell me, why have you chosen Finance? You weren't much of a geek either, if I recall well!'

'Well, almost the same reason as yours,' Aryan replied, 'except that I haven't found my career path yet. The search is on.'

'You definitely realize that you can't bank on Naina each time now to help you with your Cost Accounting assignments, right?' Vandana asked. 'You are not in the same class anymore.'

'So what? It's just another division,' I said. 'She had better continue helping me or I am screwed!'

Our discussion was interrupted by a loud and shrill "Good morning, class!". Mrs. Nilima Agrawal, or "Siren" as she was fondly called, was the self-proclaimed "know-it-all" in the world of Marketing. She could go on for at least two hours and thirty minutes about how her breakthrough ideas of marketing strategy saved X, Y and Z companies from getting a beating in the market and catapulted them to the top market position. The balance thirty minutes of the lecture she would throw open to random discussions, most of which would be limited to case examples on women's personal care products and McDonald's. Her nickname was attributed to her well-known ability to pierce her sharp sound waves right through our eardrums. However, on being informed by inside sources about the same, she had assumed an altogether different reason for her being christened "Siren" and she had almost bloated with pride.

'Hello everyone, I'll be teaching you the subjects of Consumer Behaviour and Marketing Research,' she said, measuring each and every one with her big eyes underscored by a mile wide eye-liner. I took out a brand new register and wrote down in bold: CONSUMER BEHAVIOUR: LECTURE 1, and was set to begin taking notes seriously. But Siren apparently had different plans for the day.

'So I hope all of you had a good time during your summer training?' she asked. 'You must have certainly found a new dimension to your entire MBA experience!'

The class shouted, "Yes!" in unison even as I gulped saliva. *Yes, so many dimensions I almost got lost in the maze.*

'Why don't some of you share your experiences with the class?' she said as she began to scan the classroom.

Damn it. I dug my head into my register and started flipping its pages. I ensured I didn't make eye contact with her, lest she may ask me to oblige the audience with my tales of triumph at VRF. There were over-enthusiastic geeks in the room, however, who, with their arms stretched upward, were more than willing to share their experiences. So we had a much expected *gyan* session by the students for the first half, followed by a nostalgic narration by Siren about her days in MBA, and how, as a female student in the late eighties, she fought all the conventional norms of Indian tradition and went on to be the only female member in an organization that sold sanitary napkins. Her ascent to the level that she stood at, and the grit she showed in doing so was undoubtedly admirable. But what was even more admirable was her ability to go on incessantly about her laurels.

Even as the discussion flowed, Aryan and I sat playing "dot-to-dot" in my register with total concentration. Vandana sat on my other side and exchanged paper messages with me about a possible movie plan for the evening. Naina and I exchanged text messages across classrooms even as she bitched about the snooty professor who had already given them a huge assignment in derivatives. Multitasking in the classroom during running lectures is a difficult art, and I felt proud to have mastered that art in such respects to utmost perfection.

At lunch, we got together again round the lunch table, and began catching up on all the scoops we had missed telling each other over the past two months. Everyone had their own summer stories to recount; especially Aryan, who had been trying to convince us for long that he had been lauded for his innovative idea to sell the company's latest snack item in plastic jars of different SKUs, and that he had been offered a pre-placement offer by his boss. My attention at that point of time, however, had drifted across to a very pretty face in the cafeteria. A girl, presumably from our junior batch, walked across our table and left me spellbound. She bore sharp features, a skin as shiny and smooth as ivory, and a cute dimple that ran miles deep into her adorable cheeks.

'Are you lost, Nakul?' Swapnil asked.

'Ok guys, I have just seen the eighth wonder of the world,' I declared, 'she's right here in the canteen.'

'Where? Who?' Sameer shouted, as excited as a toddler would get on seeing a jar of jelly-bellies.

'Quiet! Down, boy,' I cautioned, 'I don't want her to know we are talking about her. She's the one in the *kurta* with the orange floral print.'

All eyes turned towards my Dimple Doll in unison.

'That one?' Aryan pointed at her and shouted out loud, making things just more than obvious. Dimple Doll looked at us too. That shriek let out by Aryan was loud enough to get the entire college up on its feet. She dropped a short glance and in all probability, she saw my tomato-red face flush in embarrassment.

'You stupid monkey!' I held Aryan's collar. 'Now look what you've done!'

'Don't worry, bro, I was helping you with the PR,' he explained while trying to let go, 'Public Relations, you know! She'll now try and give you attention to find out why you give her so much attention!'

'Splendid reasoning, I must say!' I mocked.

'Seven-point-five, tops!' Naina spoke for the first time in the entire discussion.

'Huh? Seven-point-five, did you say?' I retorted. 'On what grounds do you cut two-point-five from those Picture Perfect looks?'

'Umm, eight would be good,' Sameer countered. 'But I've seen better.'

'Alright, she is Miss Universe,' Swapnil said, finally exasperated. 'Now will someone tell me what the plan is for the day?'

'We never have plans, my friend,' Aryan chuckled. 'I would be some place and someone else had I put some planning into my life!'

'Let's hit the beach then, what else,' Sameer suggested. 'Raju's *sev-puri* must be running out of business now, given that we were the only ones who ever contributed to his turnover! As it is, we've nothing to do anyway.'

'Oh no, we do have something to do,' Swapnil said with the wave of a hand.

'If it's again some questionnaire filling business for another corporate project,' Naina warned, 'I'm outta here.'

'Relax!' he smiled. 'It's something I am sure you'll like to do. It's Vandana's birthday day after tomorrow, and I was wondering if we could plan some surprise or something. I was speaking to her yesterday, and she seemed to be in the blues, because this is going to be her first birthday away from home.'

'Not a bad idea,' Sameer said, 'but booking a good restaurant or something will throw our budget out of whack.'

'Exactly,' Swapnil nodded his head, 'and moreover, there is nothing novel in booking a restaurant. It's a stale idea.'

'So what else do you suggest?' I asked.

'Our hostel terrace tomorrow at midnight...'

'Are you out of your mind, Swapnil?' I said. 'Girls are not even permitted to set foot on our hostel premises. So don't even think about it.'

'I know,' Sameer frowned, and punched his fist on the table. 'How I hate that rule! But hey, one second, there is a way out. We can always try convincing the guard. If he lets them in, it's all fine.'

'Ok,' I replied hesitatingly, 'we can try doing that.'

'Alright, done then!' Swapnil clasped his hands enthusiastically. 'Naina, you arrange for the cake and get Vandana to our hostel tomorrow midnight. Is that fine?'

Naina did not reply. She kept meddling mindlessly with her phone, looking at nothingness.

'Naina?'

'I don't know,' she said in a hassled tone, 'you guys decide whatever you have to', and walked off.

'What's with her?' Swapnil asked.

'I don't know,' I said, 'I'll go find out.'

I stopped her just before she entered a rickshaw to head back to the hostel. 'What happened to you?' I asked. 'Why

'It's nothing, I am sorry.' She mumbled. 'I have a severe headache. I need to head back to the hostel and get a nap.'

'Should I come drop you?'

'No thanks. I'll be fine.'

'Ok, I'll call you in the evening some time,' I said.

'Where did your Dimple Doll disappear?' Sameer asked as we headed back towards the library to wrap up the day's assignments.

'I don't know,' I said, craning my neck around. 'I can't seem to find her.'

'She's with a band of boys on the lawns, baby,' Aryan said.

'O hell, you don't stand a chance today, then,' Sameer patted me on the shoulder. 'Competitors loom large right now.'

'Oh yes you do,' Aryan said. 'Those guys are your juniors, remember? They hardly qualify as a threat. Let's go rag them and shoo them off.'

'Some other time, maybe,' I said. 'I got some work to do.'

I couldn't help but think about Naina at that point of time. She had never behaved that way before, and I knew for certain that it wasn't a headache that kept her down. I remembered the time when, not long ago, she had tirelessly stood by me when things were not right for me. It was my turn now to reciprocate, but I also knew she was not the kinds who would open up that easily. I couldn't hold on until evening, and sent her a text message:

Hi...I know u r upset about something...please do let me know if there is anything I can do to help.

Within seconds I got a beep on my phone.

Thanks Nakul…I am actually quite ok now…was just bogged down by some problem but am feeling much better…do u think v could go to the beach for a while in the evening if u r free?

I was far from being free that evening, with a tedious assignment on Product Marketing Strategy lined up for submission the next day. And I had already left on the professor an impression not worth boasting about, as he had caught me reading John Grisham in his class. But this was still not a tough call to take.

Sure…give me a call when u want to…I'll b there.

CHAPTER 16

A World Beyond CGPA

The sea was almost dead calm that evening, and the waves culminated almost two hundred metres ahead of where Naina and I sat. Yet the most delicate sound of the water was clearly audible, thanks to the pin drop silence that we had kept for the first half hour.

'Are you still sleepy?' I finally asked.

'No. I am fine now.'

'Then why are you so quiet?'

'I know, it's strange, we haven't spoken at all. Sing a song.'

'What?'

'You heard me. I need to get into a better mood. So sing a nice song.'

'Look here, Naina,' I said, 'I know pretty well we are not here to sing songs. So, over with it and let it out now.'

'I've been a little worried since morning,' she finally began. 'Ramchandran is creating some trouble for me in my summer project grading.'

Ramchandran, or Ramu, as most of us called him (not out of affection, but due to sheer inconvenience of pronouncing a long name) was a Finance whiz, and a professor who classified his students into two pools- the pro Ramu philosophy and the anti Ramu philosophy. While most students chose to enter the first pool out of fear of the Ramu phenomenon, there were a few adventurous ones who volunteered to register themselves for the latter, by having publicly raised questions against the fundas propounded by him. Naina happened to be one of those unfortunate scapegoats who bleated a bit too blatantly in one of his classes in the last trimester of the first year. She had gotten into his bad books already, and to add to her misfortune, he was the internal faculty assigned to guide her in her summer project, which also meant that he would be grading her project.

'What is he up to? I asked.

'He told me that my findings of the project were frivolous and based on inadequate research, and if that he were me, he wouldn't even bother to submit such an ineffective report. Imagine the wretch!'

'Hold on, take it easy,' I said, as I noticed her eyes welling up. Now that was really the last thing I wanted. And I know girls can never take it easy once they have made up their mind to cry. 'Didn't your company guide commend you on your work?' I asked.

'Face it, Nakul. Don't you know the feedback from the company is a mere formality on paper? Everything is in Ramu's hands now.'

She had begun to cry now, and I felt absolutely helpless, because I know that the feeling of realizing beforehand that your results are going to be screwed is extremely painful, and no amount of comforting can soothe your nerves then.

'Look, one thing is for sure,' I said softly, 'he can't fail you. Even the most sadistic and insane professor would not do that to a student's career. At worst, you might get a lower grade than you really deserve.'

'That isn't something insignificant to me, Nakul. Every subject's grade matters to me and to my CGPA.'

'For God's sake, Naina,' I begged, 'there is a world beyond CGPA!'

That almost sounded like a plea for reassurance for my sake. If a 3.5 plus CGPA was so concerned about what was to happen to her because of a slightly lower grade, it was high time this sub-three CGPA did something to envisage a bright future for himself.

'You don't understand,' she said. 'It's going to be a tough task for me, because my choices are very limited. I am looking for a credit rating profile, and there are going to be barely a handful of companies coming to campus for that profile. And almost the entire Finance batch will be eyeing those.'

'Look at the positive side,' I said. 'You atleast know where you want to be headed. Most of us are still groping in the dark!'

She looked at me with such a sore "don't compare me with you" look that I wished I had kept shut. I had nothing whatsoever to say beyond that. I patted her on the shoulder and took a final shot by giving the most predictable line of advice, picked straight from one of the sermons of the Holy Scriptures.

'Just have faith in yourself. Trust me, you are the best, and you're going to get the best too!'

Wow Nakul! If a certain Readers' Digest edition were to carry out a survey to rank the world's best agony counselors,

'Thanks,' she said, trying her best to put up a smile. 'I wish it were true, though.'

'Ok, even if it weren't true,' I said, 'please don't get glum about it right now. There's atleast a month to the results being declared still!'

'Easier said than done, isn't it?' she said half-mockingly.

'Do it still,' I said, 'your smile is important to your friends around you- it's important to me.'

I could hardly believe what I was saying. I had probably never said that to anyone before. But when I said that to Naina, I knew I meant every word of it.

'I am glad to hear that, Nakul,' she smiled. 'I really am.'

That smile did well to nullify the guilt of missing out on working on an important assignment because of the satisfaction I got on knowing that my presence did a bit of good to light a smile on a friend's face. We strolled around for another couple odd hours till I felt her mood was perfectly fine again.

'I got to go,' I said finally, 'there's some lousy assignment I've to submit tomorrow.'

'Yeah, it's pretty late anyway,' she said, 'let's leave.'

'I hope you're going to follow what I've told you!'

'I will,' she said, 'thanks. Good night!'

Midnight was really not an ideal time to start reading and analyzing a fifteen page case study on a new product launch, written in something like font size eight. I tried to suppress my guilt, but finally out of desperation picked Sameer's duly completed assignment and began doing what I was best at- Copy, Edit and Paste. I had a fresh assignment in my name after having changed the font style, decorating the title page and the data tables and diagrams- and crashed to bed soon after. No sooner had I fallen asleep, than I was woken up with my loud SMS beep.

Thanks a lot, Nakul. It felt great talking to you today. I am glad I have a friend like you!- Naina.

Her SMS touched a chord somewhere, so much that I kept that SMS safely stored in my archives always. It made me feel that I was of indispensable value to my friends, and I felt closer to them. My friends lay at the crux of every decision I made, and I had already begun to dread to imagine how difficult it would be to adjust without them once these two years came to an end.

Excessive attachment, however, as a good friend in engineering college often remarked, was a sweet sorrow, because much that it brought you the joy of camaraderie, it also brought along with it the sores of heightened expectations. And heightened expectations when unfulfilled, he said, begin creating chasms in relations. I could never relate to what he said, because I had never felt an attachment of that level before I met these friends at B-School. But as my attachment towards Naina grew over time, I only saw the bond grow stronger by the day- because I didn't see any situation of unfulfilled expectations arise- not until Naina herself ensured in time to come that I begin believing my friend's theory.

CHAPTER 17

The Flamingo's Flight

'No!' The grumpy guard at the hostel gate exclaimed, his eyes widening with disbelief. '*Kya bolte ho!' What are you saying!* He stood upright with his chest swelled up in an adamant posture.

'Come on, Ratan Bhai,' we pleaded, 'it's just a small birthday celebration.'

'No, no, no!' Ratan Bhai shook his head violently. 'These rules can't be broken.'

'It's her birthday today,' I said with dramatic effect, 'don't you think she deserves a party? Do you really want to deprive her of this happiness?'

Ratan Bhai's expression changed to mild sympathy for the first time in half an hour. But his intent remained firm. We continued goading him menacingly but to no avail.

'Aryan and I will go fetch the cake, as there is not much time,' Swapnil said, looking at his watch. He then leaned forward and whispered: 'I trust both of you should be able to pull this one off.'

'You bet we will!' Sameer assured him. 'You guys carry on.'

Once they left, we turned around to look at the guard again. His head continued shaking sideways with unmitigated intensity.

'Boss, please try and understand...'

'Now if you speak a word more, this matter will go to the higher authorities,' he warned. 'I have told you clearly...'

Sameer brandished a crisp five hundred rupee note in the air, and then stuffed it into Ratan's shirt pocket. He patted the guard's chest and spoke with a wide grin: 'Come on, Ratan Bhai, there is nothing that can't be resolved amongst us. I am sure we have got a deal here?'

I gawked at the guard's face in fright. I retreated a little, fearing his scruples would manifest themselves in the form of a resounding slap across one of our faces.

'*Mein Gott,* Sameer!' I gasped. 'That may not have been the wisest thing to do. He might just book us for bribery too now.'

Fortunately, nothing of the sort happened. On the contrary, Ratan mellowed down a bit. He cast us a worried glance, subdued under a sheepish smile. 'You'll have me put in trouble.' His words wavered and trembled with fear.

'Don't worry,' Sameer patted him on the shoulder, 'I have ways worked out. If anything goes wrong, it will be my neck-not yours.'

'If any of the other guys finds out, everyone will start making similar demands...'

'Nobody will find out,' Sameer smiled, 'if you let us in from behind.'

Reluctantly, Ratan led us to the rear side of the hostel, to a small awning that opened into the guard room. It was a tiny enclosure, with modicum furnishings. A damp stench filled the air in the room. A small wooden cot lay in one corner, and beside it lay a table fan with a broken blade on a tripod with a broken leg. The only ventilation for the room came through a small grilled window, that would allow sun rays during the day only sufficient to keep the room one degree below pitch darkness. And I thought of the five hundred rupee note that we conveniently stuffed into his pocket without any qualms. Insignificant as it may have seemed at the outset, it filled me later with a sense of guilt, for despite those penurious living conditions, Ratan had always carried with him a sense of pride and sincerity about his work. And with that little bribe, we had mauled his dignity and the sense of contentment he associated with his work, and that act filled me with tremendous guilt. And that day onwards, each time I would cast a glance at his dingy room contrasted by his unyielding energy when he stood at the hostel gate under the blazing sun all day long, that dagger of guilt would stab hard at my conscience.

We found our way up to the terrace through a thin spiral wooden staircase beginning from Ratan's room. The wood had peeled off the corners of the stairs and they yielded an abnormally loud creaking sound with each step we placed on them. The staircase moaned aloud under the pressure of my abundant mass, and I feared a bad fall lest it would give way. We ambled up as fast as possible to the top, till we reached a cobweb-decorated iron door that opened into the rear side of the terrace. The patio boasted of elaborate arrangements that would suit a grand celebration. A laptop was placed on a table at the side, fitted to a pair of speakers. The decision to bring in music with speakers was taken after due deliberation, given the possibility of attracting unsolicited attention from the other students in the hostel. But then again, the plan was a calculated one. Being just the beginning of the new academic year after summers, a number of students had taken an extended vacation after training and had not returned from home. Moreover, that happened to be a Friday night, which meant a good number of guys had either hit the movie hall for the latest film in town, or were out clubbing or pub-ing. That left only the geeks in the hostel, who were anyway likely to remain in the confines of their rooms, and would be least bothered about the jamboree that was to take place on the terrace post midnight. Aryan and I had sat laboriously through the afternoon, burning a compilation of the choicest songs from our music library. Pizza packets from Domino's were stacked up on a separate table, and beside the stack lay a crate of premium vodka and whisky bottles, handpicked by Sameer. And, of course, right in the centre of the table was what completed the definition of a grand festivity: a scrumptious chocolate truffle cake with the most exquisite icing that Aryan and Swapnil brought from the cake shop. All these and four hungry stomachs waited eagerly for the two girls to arrive.

'How long are they going to take?' I groaned in hunger.

'They should be here in ten minutes,' Swapnil said, 'Naina sent a message saying they just left from their hostel.'

When a delectable treat tantalizes you at an arm's distance without allowing you to touch it, sending your gut into writhing bouts of pain, the wait is a ceaseless one. Ten minutes seemed like eons even as we watched the chocolate cream gleam seductively under the candle lit on the cake. The aroma of the chocolate and the molten cheese coming from the pizza packets filled my senses, and hunger clawed hard at my stomach. The pain persisted until the girls finally arrived.

'The pleasantries will happen later,' Aryan said, pulling Vandana towards the table, and thrusting a bread knife into her hand. 'First please do the needful.'

Our eyes widened involuntarily in a lecherous stare as Vandana's bread knife made its way slowly through the depth of the succulent dessert. No sooner than the cake was cut, than we all plunged ourselves into it. Within no time, we had consumed every molecule of it, and had begun licking the cream off all corners of the empty cardboard box.

'That was a good start,' I said happily, smacking my fingers, 'now should we serve the pizzas too?'

'Not so soon,' Sameer declared, raising his hand to stop me, 'I have different plans for us.' He heaved the crate of vodkas and whiskies towards the circle we had formed on the floor where we sat.

'Pick one each, each one of you,' Sameer said, laying special emphasis on the latter part of his command while casting a meaningful glance at me. 'Let all resolutions be violated tonight!'

Swapnil and I looked at each other hesitantly. 'I'm sorry, Sameer,' I said, 'you know I won't!'

'Come on, man,' Sameer coaxed me, 'just this once. Do it for us-for the sake of friendship!'

For the sake of friendship. Considering how highly I had come to place my association with these friends over a year's span, I found this phrase effective enough to get me to do anything - absolutely anything under the sun. Joining them for a drink at their behest seemed like a trifle. Of course, there is little logical connection between faith in a relation and tasting alcohol. But then, as I believed, friendship never thrives on logic.

'Alright then, this is for you, Vandana,' I nodded at her, raising my bottle up in a toast, 'here goes nothing!' I put the bottle of vodka to my mouth and helped myself to a rather large swig. It was a bad way for a novice to begin. Firstly, my stomach was already on fire owing to the hours of hunger I had sustained. Secondly, I had not had the gumption to realize the difference between drinking vodka and drinking cola. As the liquid found its place in the empty ravines of my body, I felt an intense heat surge up within me. I moaned, coughed and spluttered. Aryan and Sameer grinned mischievously into my face.

'You had it neat, you dork!' Sameer hooted. 'Here, let me make it nicer for you.' He poured the vodka out into an empty glass till quarter of its level, and filled up the rest of the glass with Sprite. 'Here, this should be good. Cheers!'

The consistency of the drink was mellowed, but the quantity kept increasing. My glass was refilled for the second round, and in spite of myself, I gratefully accepted it again - for the sake of friendship. I could feel I was beginning to lose control gradually, but somehow I did not fight much to stop myself.

There are definite moments at certain stages in our lives that, for no apparently significant reason, leave with us an endearing memory - like a drug that we crave for in the future again and again. That night, as I leaned back groggily against the parapet wall of the terrace and gazed idly at the night sky, I found that moment transform into that drug I would crave for ceaselessly, time and again. There was a hue of pink spread across, signifying the arrival of the monsoon. The familiarly affable smell of sand dampened with the first drops of light rain filled the air. There was no sound barring the mild, soulful music that flirted with the serenity of the hour. For half an hour, there was no dialogue exchanged- just the presence of five friends whom I loved with my whole heart. I needed nothing else then, and I knew it. And in that half an hour of silence, I felt myself living a thousand lives of sheer bliss.

'I want to thank you guys,' Vandana spoke finally, bringing me back to the moment. 'This act of affection means a lot to me, trust me! I had expected this to be one of the drabbest birthdays, being away from home. But without any exaggeration, you have all made up perfectly.'

'The pleasure's all ours,' Swapnil said, giving her a bear hug. 'This was the least we thought we could do.'

'I remember having mentioned to Nakul how homesick I had felt in the initial days when I came to Mumbai,' Vandana continued, referring to the midnight discussion we had had one night outside Velocity. 'But I somehow feel very smug, very much at home when I am with you all. It's just the perfect friendship I could not have imagined I would find.'

It almost felt like she had read my thoughts aloud. I looked at her and smiled, and was just about to respond, when Naina cut in, shaking her head fervently.

'I know where you are coming from, Vandana,' she said, 'but there is a little piece of unsolicited advice I must give you. Rating any friendship as perfect is potentially one of the worst hazards you can cause to your peace of mind and state of happiness in the long run. Because just like all other things, no friendship is perfect either. Perfect friendships and perfect relationships are Utopian phenomena.'

'Whoa! That was a super line!' Aryan exclaimed. 'Utopian phenomena! Where did you pick that one from?'

'I didn't pick it, it's mine!' Naina defended. 'I tend to give vent to my artistic abilities at times too!'

'But I don't get the point, Naina,' I said after a while, 'as to why should we even be discussing all this? I mean, I don't know about you, but as far as I am concerned, I have never had better friends, and I don't think it could ever get better. Now where does your philosophy of Utopia fit in?'

'I think you have got me wrong, Nakul,' Naina said, 'when I said this, it did not mean that I love any of you any less than what you do. All that I meant was that the time that we all have shared or are going to share between us, and the bonding which we believe we have nurtured between us in this time, does not really constitute the A to Z of our lives. Tomorrow there will be more such moments, more associates, and more friends. And then more. Of what we share between ourselves today, there will be only memories we will have to latch on to.' She raised her glass in her hand and continued, 'So guys, live this night while it lasts, but don't make this your lifeline!'

I looked at her closely. I was three quarters down, felt tipsy and could not see much too clearly. But I could surely study that unmistakable firmness in her eyes as she spoke. 'How many have you had?' I nudged her and winked.

'Huh?'

'How many have you had?' I showed her my glass, clinking at its surface with my fingers.

'Quite a few,' she giggled, 'but hey, not enough to not know what I am talking, ok? I meant every word of what I just said, and I will mean it tomorrow too!'

'Ok!' I smiled at her, pushing myself back to lean against the parapet wall again. It was a forceful, unintended smile, fractured somewhere by the bluntness of her remarks. There was nothing new that she said that I had not heard before. But the effortless candour with which she made those remarks diluted the divinity of the relation I believed I shared with her. I opened that little window of my memories and revived those instances where she had spoken aloud in her honest voice what her friendship with me meant to her. That honesty in her voice and eyes could not fail me. But then what did her remarks mean? Were those instances also mere fleeting fads for her, only the memories of which she would latch on to? Leaving several such questions unattended to, I gave her honesty the benefit of doubt. I simply looked at her and smiled again. 'I think you *have* had enough, Naina!'

'So have you, buddy!' I felt someone say to me. I looked to my left and saw Swapnil wrap his arm around my shoulder. 'I suggest you put this down now.'

He took the glass away from my hand and put it on the floor. I turned around and looked at him. He grinned his typical grin from ear to ear. His face was stone cold sober.

'You didn't drink?' I asked. He shook his head, and grinned wider.

'*Saala,* ditcher!' I mistimed an attempted punch in his stomach. 'I thought Sameer asked us to raise a toast to our friendship?'

'Yes, he did,' Swapnil smiled, 'but I did not think it necessary to drink to show that I was committed to that toast!'

'What?'

'You heard what Naina said, right? Don't make friendship your lifeline. If I can't make it my lifeline, how do you think I can let it be something that substitutes my identity? I do not drink, and I never will. And I trust my friends enough to know that my not raising a toast can't affect my friendship with them.'

'Shit, man,' I said, my head lowered, laughing embarrassedly, 'I feel like such a jerk now!'

'Whatever,' he patted me, 'just make sure you remember this for the future!'

'Okie-dokie...' My voice trailed off as I drifted into semi-sleep, until I was woken with a jolt by a voice.

'Wake up, boy! We need to talk!'

'Eh?' I looked around dreamily. The others were all stretched out on the floor, either asleep or chatting amongst themselves. I looked around again, but could not spot the source of the voice. 'Who are you?'

'You need not care about that,' said The Voice, 'you only need to listen to me.'

I was stunned. I strained my eyes open and sat back straight, looking in the direction of The Voice.

'So you are having a good time, huh?' The Voice spoke.

'Yeah, it's been fun.' I said hesitantly, unsure of where this was going.

'Hmm, nice. So, what do you think about what your friends just told you?'

'I don't think much about those comments. Naina anyway did not know what she was saying, I am sure. She was sloshed.'

'Well, is it? I think she was quite in her senses, and she made perfect sense and logic. Now it's a different thing if you want to convince yourself otherwise.'

'Well, even if it made perfect sense and logic, I shouldn't care. As someone rightly said, pure logic is the ruin of the spirit!'

'Crap! The spirit, in fact, thrives on pure logic. And the spirit that does not follow logic strays into an endless, gloomy black hole.'

'Alright.'

'What's alright?'

'I mean, thanks for your uncalled for sermon. But my spirit is smug and happy thriving on sentiment rather than logic, and I wouldn't want to change the way it functions.'

'Ok, if you insist. But do remember, no friendship is worth making your lifeline.'

'Alright, I have heard that in some ten different ways in the last half hour or something. Now, if you don't mind,' I snapped, 'I really like this song, and would appreciate some silence.' I crawled, almost on all fours, towards the music system, and turned the volume knob higher as the song switched to Roger Waters' *Comfortably Numb.*

'Hmm, *Comfortably Numb*! Do you know the significance of the phrase?'

'What phrase?'

'*Comfortably Numb*, dunderhead!'

'Well, I am not sure. Maybe I do, or maybe I don't.'

'Even if you don't, you will, some day: the day you realize what I said; the day you contend with your friend's opinion.'

'What's that?'

'That no friendship is worth making your lifeline. The day when you realize, that at the end, when you look around you, you are all alone. That day will you not only understand the phrase, but also feel it.'

The Voice was gone. I made some effort and stood up on my feet and looked around. He was gone. A few steps away, I watched Sameer haul Vandana up and dance a jig with her, while the others looked on and clapped merrily. I smiled to myself and joined them in the circle. For a few seconds, my mind kept wandering back to the phrase "Comfortably Numb". *At the end, when you look around you, you are all alone.* But the words evaporated soon. That night, in that most memorable night of those two years, I smiled my biggest smile. That night, my heart was a flamingo, and it flapped away, high up in the Utopian skies.

CHAPTER 18

Dimple Doll Again

We walked down the corridor the next morning and came across a large notice posted on the board: Management Education Faculty, New Delhi, invites participation for the annual inter-college agri-business plan contest to be held on the 4th of September. Preliminary entries of the business plan to be submitted by the 3rd of August, 2005. Individual participation only. Log on to www.mefcontests.com for details.

Aryan and I were thrilled to read the news. We finally saw an opportunity that could convince us that there was more to us than biting our fingernails off during term exams, strumming Coldplay and Jagjit Singh on the beach in the dead of the night, and getting subdued by an ugly phenomenon called CGPA. We went straight to the library and scanned the website for more information:

"Viable Business Plans For Rural Market In India".

Rural India today, is in no way behind other industries in terms of adoption of latest technology and infrastructure for its business. Online rural marketing has opened up a window to rural India, ruling out the myth that Indian villages may not be able to withstand the force of rapid changes in information technology. With this scenario in view, and the way it is expected to evolve in the future, and factoring in consumer insights and market dynamics, you are expected to chart out a business plan that is financially viable and sustainable for profit-making organizations.

The business plan should be sent in a soft copy of no more than 5000 words, inclusive of an executive summary.

I knew from the word "go" that the work needed a level of zest and commitment I had failed to show in anything I did that far in life. But with little time left for placements, the pressure of adding up to our credentials was mounting by the day.

'It's now or never,' Aryan and I kept reminding each other.

With no past experience in writing a contest paper, I did not even know the structure and content that was expected of me. Like on many other past occasions, I had a ready solution in my elder sister who also, a few years before me, had done her MBA, with the sole difference being that she had been the topper of her batch. This difference, much to my annoyance, was a metric of comparison between the two of us each time my parents had to remind me that I needed to mend my ways.

'A business plan must be such that the end benefit can justify the time, effort and money invested into it,' my sister began in highly theoretical fashion. 'There's a host of factors one needs to take into account while conceptualizing a b-plan.'

I scribbled down the required check-points at the other end of the phone.

- ❑ Value chain analysis
- ❑ Market analysis and strategy

- Financial implications
- Infrastructure and Logistics requirement
- Socio-cultural and legal forces of influence
- Risks and contingency plans…

'Ok, this is done,' I heaved a sigh. 'What next?'

'What's next is obviously that you have to use these points as the base for your business plan,' she said. 'Prepare a plan after factoring in each of these points. I think this is what they are looking for.'

I started collecting all the data I could, put two and two together, and tried to make good business sense. Much that Sameer was himself busy with a corporate project he had taken up in retail banking, he voluntarily sat with Aryan and me and gave us a few pointers we could use. We both sat like two tenacious workers, resolving to shed the black sheep image off our back once and for all. We promised ourselves not to lift our otherwise fidgety butts off the chair until we at least had a plan on table.

'Do you think bunking the afternoon lecture was a bad idea?' Aryan asked after the lecture had actually ended. 'We are already pretty low on attendance.'

'It hardly matters,' I replied, 'we have attended enough lectures during the first year and have seen their yield too.'

'Actually you are right,' Aryan concurred, 'and anyway, Swapnil must've taken care of the proxy thing!'

Swapnil was one person we could always count on for two things: One, that he would never bunk a single lecture, even if that meant walking straight out of bed to make it in time for the nine o clock lecture without taking a shower-which in turn ensured that we had ready notes to study from for each subject before a trimester exam. The second was that Swapnil always made sure none of his friends got troubled by petty nuisances like giving explanations for not fulfilling the eighty percent attendance requirement.

We walked out to catch a bite and a breath of fresh air. The lawns had a sizable chunk of the junior junta seated in a circle with an empty Coke bottle in between, playing the all-favourite pastime of "Truth-n-Dare". Seeing them instantly reminded me of the initial days when I had just begun to know my friends, and for the first time actually realized the essence of the saying that "time flies fast". *We have less time now together than what we've already spent! And it still feels like it has just begun!* Much that we often wished to sit again in the lawns idly and share a light moment or two together, we had all begun to feel things change around us. Exchanging wisecracks and passing chits on the last bench of the class was now a rarity; we now sat in class mostly to get pointers that could help us get well-equipped with our "domain knowledge" as Sameer called it. Our time in the library was less spent on chatting through the local messenger service than preparing for and participating in the n number of inter-college contests. Aryan's guitar strings had begun to rust away from lack of use, save a few occasions here and there when the beach would beckon us. Sameer and Swapnil had busied themselves with their respective corporate projects too, and our late night "discussions" on the hostel terrace had become infrequent. The case with Naina and Vandana was worse yet, as they would be visible on campus only during class hours, confining themselves mostly to their hostel for the rest of the time. Vandana would still, sometimes, find time out once in a while if she was insisted upon. But the phantom of placements had started looming big time over Naina's mind, and convincing her to spare some time out when she felt she didn't have any, was a task we were all incapable of handling.

'Someone needs to tell them to invest their time wisely,' Aryan said, stirring me from my thoughts. 'There are some people here from whose experiences they can learn!'

'It's hardly a big deal, Aryan,' I said, 'it's good, in fact, that we also made the most of the first year, given that things are going to be tight hereon till the placements happen.'

'You mean our vacation period is over?' Aryan asked.

'For now, yes it is,' I said, 'till the placements. But we've got three months more after that. We'll party hard!'

'Amen to that!' said Aryan. 'Now let's eat.'

We walked over to the *Dilip Dosa-n-Sandwich* stall outside the college gate, which, at any given hour of the day, had a heavy deluge of customers from our and other nearby colleges. His snacks were quite a rage among all the students, and this business had, over the past decade, raised him from a mere sandwich vendor to a high-flying businessman. He was also now the proud owner of a shiny grey Hyundai Accent which he drove to work in the morning. A transition from selling *dabelis* at two rupees a piece to being the most sought after sandwich outlet owner in suburban Vile Parle, Dilip was a live case study of successful market expansion and growth strategy. I often contemplated joining him in his business in a worst case scenario of not landing up a good clinch in the placements.

'Two jam-cheese toasts, Dilip Uncle! Please make it fast.'

It was a warm, sunny afternoon. We stood under the shade of the thatched roof of the stall, and looked around at the multitude of students throng the various stalls in the same line. And there, in the huge crowd, there was one face that shone distinctly brighter than the others. At the adjacent stall stood Dimple Doll, with the radiance of her skin second only to the blaze of the afternoon sun. She stood barely ten feet away with a plate of some weird looking dosa- chilly dosa probably, but I hardly cared to notice that. She looked flawlessly beautiful, just like the first time we had seen her in the café. She wore a light lavender top and a long printed skirt in a multitude of colours. And while I am not a big fan of multi-coloured outfits, even the most outrageous outfit could not possibly affect the impeccability of her appearance. She seemed to be having a tough time with the spice in her food, even as her little nose began to turn ruddy red from the corners, and beads of sweat began trickling down her temples. Instinctively, I mustered some gall and walked up to her with my jam-cheese toast in my hand.

'Too spicy, huh?'

She gave me a half-puzzled, half-stern look; a typical reaction expected on being greeted by a stranger-especially if the stranger made it obvious he was hitting on her. Vandana often said that girls could immediately tell if a guy was coming on too fast, and I, despite my best efforts, was just substantiating her statement here.

'I am Nakul, by the way,' I stretched my hand forward, 'from your senior batch. And that's my friend Aryan.'

'Hi, I'm Ruchi Karwal.' Her eyes were beginning to get watery now.

As she placed her palm in mine, in a perfect handshake, I found the tenderness strike a rude contrast against the rough surface of my palms. There were calluses formed on my fingertips over years of unsuccessful attempts at mastering my skill with the cricket bat, and it embarrassed me, in fact, almost made me feel guilty of hurting that perfect skin with the roughness of my hands.

'Here, try a bite of this,' I said, extending my plate of jam-cheese toast towards her. 'It might soothe you down.'

'No thanks,' she politely declined. 'I'm done. I'll be fine now.'

As she went a few steps further to make her payment, Aryan leaned over my shoulder and whispered, 'Easy, boy! That much is enough for the first meeting!'

'So, how goes the first trimester?' I asked, ignoring Aryan's warning. That was the blandest of topics I could've initiated, but I was short of matter then.

'Uh, it's ok, I guess,' she said, 'it's just begun, though. Let's see how it goes further. Is the grind too bad?'

'Well, in certain ways, yes,' I went on, 'the load can get on to you at times. But at the end of the day it's all about time management. You just need to balance your other activities with your academic requirements.'

Aryan almost let out a short snigger. I couldn't blame him, because I myself felt funny preaching time management to others. But this was one of those rare occasions where I felt the need to sound scholarly.

'Yeah, Nakul has epitomized time management for us,' Aryan retorted in an obvious tone of mockery. 'You could learn a lesson or two from him in that regard!'

'Alright, now I get it!' She laughed.

'Anyway, we got to go, we are a bit rushed,' Aryan said, 'see you later again.'

'Oh sure,' she said, 'bye.'

Damn it! A bit rushed for what?

'What's your problem, bozo?' I shouted at Aryan as we moved forward. 'What was the big rush for? We had just got talking!'

'Dude, easy does it,' Aryan replied, 'you need to play "hard-to-get" here.'

'What the...?'

'I mean it. If you like a girl, the last thing you want to do is to make it so damn obvious that she can see right through,' he said. 'Man, I wish you could first take a few pointers from Sameer regarding this. You're still raw at the game.'

'First things first,' I clarified. 'I'm not interested in her. Alright, she's gorgeous, but that doesn't mean I must go running after her. I was just socializing...'

'Socializing my foot! You were almost bent upon stuffing that toast into her mouth!'

'Aw, shut up now,' I said, 'let's get back to work. We've a great deal to do on that case yet.'

We walked back to the library, which wasn't exactly an exhilarating feeling after having had a nice, long break. But the work had to be done nonetheless, so we sat through another session of dogged research and collation of data, till it was almost dinnertime.

'What plans?' I asked. 'I am bored.'

'I wish I could say that too,' Aryan sighed, 'but I've got some crazy assignment in Financial Institutions and Markets to be submitted this week. And it's one devil of an assignment!'

'O drat! I've taken that subject too! What was this assignment all about, I can't seem to remember.'

'Some stuff on ledgers or things like that. I don't remember. I am as bright in this field as you are!'

I laughed. 'Yeah, I think it's our brightness that binds us together! Am I proud of us!'

It was said then in passing jest, but it was indeed the truth and both of us knew it. Our lanes of fate had twisted and turned at precisely equal angles throughout our journey, and had stayed parallel throughout. We had tasted disappointment and failure together, and in time to come, were to find reasons to celebrate together too. At all points of trough, together we had learnt to laugh at our misfortunes, and together we had learnt to wade out of them each time. Whether our association grew stronger by this mutual need, or because of mutual admiration for each other, never mattered to any of us. What mattered was that the definition of a true friend, if ever such a definition existed, was epitomized by him. And that definition never failed me. It somehow managed to stand the test of time, even after most other beliefs I once harboured got diffused somewhere down the line in time.

CHAPTER 19

An Insignificant Dream

A heavy downpour forcing the cancellation of an afternoon lecture on "Financial Institutions and Markets" was seemingly the best thing that could happen that day.

'Thank God!' I said. 'I'd not finished my assignment.'

'You never do anyway,' Naina mocked, 'you always have me complete them for you!'

'Whoever invented terms like bookkeeping and ledgers? Why the hell did I even decide to take Finance as a minor?'

'Stop asking yourself questions now. The underlying message is that you need to work on your Finance subjects.'

'Ok, stop being a preacher. And tell me, you had promised to help me on this assignment, Brutus! Where were you on Saturday anyway? I messaged you; you didn't even bother to reply.'

'I'm sorry about that,' she said rather casually, 'Vandana and I had gone out with a few friends from my Finance class. We were down town the whole day, movie and dinner. We returned late that night, so I may have forgotten to reply.'

'What movie?'

'*Salaam Namaste.* And I'll tell you what, Saif looked super!'

I paused for a minute and looked at her in dismay. 'You watched it already? I told you we were planning it together, right? I had spoken to you about this the same morning, *yaar*! And you didn't even bother to tell us?'

'O man, I forgot, I'm sorry! Anyway, you guys must go catch it now.'

'You're missing the point, Naina. We were free almost the whole of last weekend. You could have at least told us you had separate plans with the Finnies so that we could have gone ahead.'

Finnies was the collective noun I had coined for Naina and her bunch of geeky friends from the Finance division. I don't think I ever found out their names; I never got close enough to them to consider it important to know their names. I had managed instead throughout by referring to them as The Finnies.

'Listen, I said I am sorry, didn't I?' She said, raising her voice. 'The Finnies planned it at the last moment and asked us to join them. I just forgot to ask you. Now will you stop making a big deal out of this?'

Big deal? Now that pricks pretty badly!

'Ok, I will.' I said quietly, and began to walk away.

'Ok listen, I am sorry for blowing my top. It's just that I thought you are being unreasonable.'

'When you already know I was unreasonable, you don't need to apologize.' I snubbed her back.

'Ok, I'm sorry about the whole thing. I swear I am.'

'Ok. Just let's not talk about it for some time. I need to purge it out.'

It was true. I was being unreasonable and I knew it all the while I cribbed that afternoon. They had all the freedom to plan whatever they wanted to, and I was no authority in questioning them if they did so. Yet, there lay a reason to be unreasonable, a reason that could neither be defined nor justified. Maybe because reason and emotion have never thrived in the same heart. And my heart had let in so much emotion that it could accommodate nothing more. And for the first time that day, as I read through the casual, almost indifferent look on her face, I felt pretty disturbed because of that emotion. For the first time, I felt sick and disgusted. And that was just the beginning of the wreckage of all positive beliefs I ever nurtured.

There are instances like these that appear trivial at the outset. But one derives insinuations from them, magnifies them and indents them on the walls of one's heart. After the first indent, the walls are weakened, and the heart is exposed to every minute instance thereon, and to the implication it forcefully fetches out of it. Each instance is mild in its individual intensity, but the aggregate of all over a period of time fills your heart with so much hate and pain, that the heart forgets to love.

'You are not angry with me, *na*?' Naina asked, tugging at my shirt sleeve.

That is the problem. Every such instance is always followed by an assurance that forces you to take a second opinion on the negative chain of thoughts that you had allowed to enter your mind only a minute back. Her question, and the perfect innocence that showed on her face as she asked me that question, made me antagonize my own insinuation. Maybe

I was being too judgemental. Maybe it was my self-created parameters of a perfect friendship that I was trying to benchmark her against. Maybe it was *my* excessive attachment the reflection of which I desperately searched for in her behaviour.

'No, I am not angry, Naina.' I said, unsure of whether that was the truth. 'Now let's go down and get some coffee.'

'Yeah, I need one. I've got a severe headache.'

The rain wasn't ready to cease just yet. It had been pouring for more than six hours now, and it looked like there was a lot more to go. The power supply had got cut off, and the cafeteria had been shut down. The premonition for the day ahead grew scarier as we saw streams of water jetting into the building premises gradually, but a larger part of the crowd remained oblivious for long to the possible extent of damage that was in store. Students let the kindergarten element out of their system, and began kicking and splashing in the rain, even as the water rose to knee-deep levels. Hungry and coffee-deprived souls like us sat in the dark library, wondering how long the wait was going to be before we could feed ourselves some food.

'I need a coffee desperately, guys!' Naina cried. 'My head's about to split!'

'Forget the coffee, what do we do about a hungry stomach?' I said. 'There's no food!'

'Same here,' Sameer and Vandana concurred. 'We haven't eaten since morning.'

'There should be biscuits available at the grocery store outside,' Swapnil suggested. 'Go get some before that also closes down.'

Determined to get our hands on some food, Sameer and I rolled up our khakis above knee-length and ventured out into something we thought was a much smaller ordeal than what actually lay ahead. We trudged along till the gate, trying to carefully place each step on terra firma. The cold rain continued lashing mercilessly at our bodies, and blurred our vision beyond eight feet ahead of us. The water level, meanwhile, kept inching its way up towards our waist.

'Damn! My khakis are going to get ruined!' Sameer said.

I was just about to look down and examine my trousers as we walked out of the gate that all of a sudden, both of us were pulled down into the water as we descended the sloped flooring of the campus.

'Ok,' I said, 'we mustn't even try and see what's happened to our khakis now!'

We walked with all our might to the grocery store.

'Uncle, three Pure Magic packets, please!' We called out to the shopkeeper, who was just about to pull the shutter down. He looked around at us in astonishment, watching two insane gluttons standing in front of his store demanding biscuits in waist-deep dirty water, even as passers-by and stranded car drivers scooted around, looking for safe refuge. He reluctantly climbed up a stool and fetched us our biscuits. I held out a hundred-rupee note.

'I can't tender you change at the moment,' he shrugged. 'My cash drawer is under water. Pay me tomorrow.'

We started walking back at twice the speed. The water wasn't anything but soothing to the bones, and we were beginning to feel really cold by now. I carefully held the biscuits under my shirt, as getting them wet would be the last thing I'd want at that time.

'What took you so long?' Naina asked as soon as we walked into the library.

'Why the hell are you still in here?' I asked them in disbelief. The library had become a miniature swimming pool, and the room had become a dingy, stinky mess. 'Let's go out.'

The thin corridor of the main building harboured more than three hundred frustrated students and faculty members, waiting for a glimmer of hope that could take them back home. But all hope was shattered when news was relayed within minutes from then that a red alert had been sounded in most parts of the city, where the water level had crossed five feet in height. Mumbai was flooded, and there appeared no respite.

'Aryan's lucky he didn't come to college,' I said. 'At least he must have something in the hostel to eat!'

'Oh shit!' Vandana exclaimed after a pause. 'He had gone to the airport this afternoon to meet a friend who was on a transit flight. I hope he's not got stuck there!'

Our jaws dropped. We took turns at trying to call him, but all phone lines had gone bust, which also meant that we all would have a set of extremely anxious parents back home, who would have freaked out by then on seeing the visuals on the news channels and on hearing the conveniently over-hyped, sensationalized information provided by the media.

Meanwhile, it was learnt that a school bus carrying some sixty to seventy young kids had got stranded right outside the college gate and the bus driver had called for assistance. In an instant, a huge bunch of students from our college rushed out, each student carrying one child to safety in a room on the top floor. Managing and entertaining a classroom of petrified kids was tough work. But it was handled beautifully nonetheless by the students. There were kids aged five and six, who were crying relentlessly, demanding that they be taken home. We sat with them, tried to make them laugh, tried to tell them some stories, but nothing seemed to work. The main problem was probably the lack of food and water, and added to that the dampness around that upset everyone. I could have almost cried out myself due to hunger.

Food came in only hours later, thanks to a few good neighbours living across the street. A few packets of bread and biscuits, and two big bottles of mineral water did not make for a lavish meal between four to five hundred hungry people, but at that point of time getting even this much was comforting. By then quite a few children had happily reunited with their parents and left, but there were still hundreds of mouths to feed. The food was first distributed among the children, after which we made do with the remainder. Our bellies may not have been full that night, but it gave us a queer feeling of satisfaction on seeing that we had done a fine job that day. When teary-eyed parents smiled at us in gratitude, I felt exultant, because my action had positively mattered to someone that day. Our value in society had been upped, and this time the driving force was neither that coveted degree nor that job to die for.

By midnight, most children had been found and taken back home. A few still stayed, though, and we braved that night with them-more than a hundred of us in a damp, dark classroom swarmed with mosquitoes and soiled with dirty water. We forced ourselves down on the cold, wet floor and tried to get some sleep.

I lie in the pool with my eyes shut, oblivious to the weather that forebodes an ugly day ahead. All of a sudden, a strong gush of wind topples me off my floating tube, and I fall face first into the icy cold water. Like all heavy objects, my portly body is no exception, and I begin going down under. I gasp for breath even as I try to keep my head above water, and call out to my friends for help. Naina and Vandana are by the poolside, but appear too busy to respond. Naina shakes Vandana hard by the shoulder and asks her to hurry up. 'We're getting late,' she shows Vandana the watch. I shout for help again, this time at the top of my voice. She finally turns to me rather indifferently. 'Yeah?'

'Help me out!' I plead.

'We're going down town and are running late,' she says, 'my friends are already waiting there. You don't worry, just hang in there. Aryan should be on his way soon.'

'I think that's utterly selfish of you,' I say.

'Listen, stop being a kid, Nakul. That rope is right on your side. You can hold on to it and come out on your own too. So please don't make a big deal out of this...'

She's right. There is a rope tied to a lamp-post right outside the pool, and the free end of the rope is within my reach. But now an emotion called anger has superimposed the emotion of fear. They disappear, leaving me in the lurch. The pool gradually turns into a quicksand, and I am being sucked in real fast. I can either keep waiting for someone to lean forth and give me a hand and get consumed by the mire in the meantime, or I need to find a way out on my own. I need to act fast. Real fast...

'Guys, my phone has come alive!' I was woken up in the morning with a start by Vandana's loud exclamation. Beads of sweat ran down my collar bone. I continued feeling snuffed for a few moments more till I was entirely awake.

'What's wrong?' Vandana looked at me, puzzled.

'Nothing,' I said, 'just a bad dream.'

'What was it?'

'Nothing, forget it. It was…insignificant.'

I walked to the classroom window and looked outside. The rain had finally stopped, and the water level had begun to recede thanks to a low sea tide that morning. But the recession was very slow, and one could still see people wade through waist-deep water. Fishermen had towed their boats onto the road, and like good Samaritans they ferried fellow civilians across some otherwise inaccessible patches in the area.

All the school children had left by then, much to our relief as well as to their own relief, and of course, most to the relief of their worried parents. We also took turns at calling our respective homes using Vandana's phone, as hers was the only phone that had become operational till then. Our phone services continued to remain disrupted. More than competitive tariff rates and fancy monthly schemes, it was testing times like these that judged a telecom service's goodness, and here Vandana's service provider emerged a clear winner.

'Aryan's fine too,' Vandana announced, 'I just got his message. He stayed in a bakery shop at night with some workers. He says he "managed" with a few pastries and patties!'

'Oh wow!' Naina said. 'You'd wish you'd be in his place, wouldn't you, Nakul?'

I didn't respond. I just didn't feel like. I looked out of the window.

'What's wrong?' Naina came up to me and asked. 'You look disturbed.'

'It's nothing. I'm fine.' I lied.

'Can I trust it's nothing to do with our not telling you about the movie on Saturday?'

I looked at her and gave a half-smile. *Some friends can see right through, can't they?*

'If you know everything, why do you even ask?'

She sighed. 'So it *is* something to do with that! Look Nakul, I said I am sorry, didn't I?'

'Hey you don't have to be sorry, you know,' I said, 'but to be honest, I was a little surprised that you could actually forget! I mean, I never forget to tell you about the smallest of plans anyone of us makes!'

'Nakul, remember one ground principle,' she said, 'no two friends are alike. Please don't expect me to be able to be like you always. I may be a little callous when it comes to matters like these, but it doesn't make me care for you less, does it?'

'No, it doesn't,' I said quietly.

'Please get this out of your mind,' she said, 'for I've seen little issues like these turning friendships sour. And I consider your friendship too special to allow it to be affected by such trifles.'

'Don't worry,' I assured her, lying again, 'this was hardly something to discuss so much about. Case dismissed!'

I may have laughed the matter off, but it continued to prick me. Does someone who doesn't figure in your top-of-mind recall for a weekend plan still continue to be a "special" friend? Is it unfair to expect even your best of friends to be what you want them to be? I shelved all such unanswered questions and tried to put my "insignificant" dream of the previous night out of my memory archives.

CHAPTER 20

Conditional Love

'I don't want to leave Mumbai,' said a one-quarter-down Sameer, 'there's no place like this! And there are no friends like you!'

'It's time for another quarter, I guess!' Aryan waved Sameer's empty glass in front of him. 'The poet's coming out of you!'

'Shut up, guys!' Sameer said defiantly. 'Every time I start saying something truly from my heart, you screw my mood with your ridicule!'

'Ok, sorry,' I said, 'but first ask for those nachos. Swapnil and I can't keep sitting and watch both of you booze.'

Sameer waved his hand at the waiter and beckoned him. 'One bowl of nachos with salsa dip, please. And yeah, two glasses of cold chocolate milk for my two friends here - with two straws!' He let out a raucous laugh. He always felt highly amused at the fact that we abstained from all forms of alcohol. In fact, he had almost felt sorry for coaxing me into drinking the other night on Vandana's birthday. We never drank, yet we could safely claim we had a frequency equivalent to that of the regulars of going to the city pubs on these drinking binges, simply because these sessions gave us long hours to sit and talk things that we wouldn't otherwise get to talk about amidst our crazy schedules of the day where we inched our way towards our ambitions.

'So, you were mentioning something about Mumbai?' Aryan reminded Sameer.

'Yeah, I am in love with near about everything about this city - the beaches, the lanes and roads, the reclamation, the local trains. And yes, also our college. I mean, yeah, I was really unimpressed when I saw it for the first time, but I have come to love it, too.'

'Ditto to everything else you said except the college thing,' Aryan said. 'There is still some time before I can come to love this place. I only hope it happens before I graduate from here. Because so far, the only memories I can attach with the college are the sleepless, nervous nights I have spent before exams and the hopeless feeling I get each time our results are out!'

'Why so?' I asked. 'I thought your grades have begun to improve, haven't they?'

'O yeah? They have improved alright. I have upgraded from a GPA of 2.78 to a GPA of 2.82. Now you can call that an improvement if you please. But to my parents, at least, I am still the same good-for-nothing dodo whose biggest achievement even remotely related to academics was a full score in a spelling test in kindergarten. Since then, I have never been something they could really be proud of. And ever since, each time any examination results are declared, I get to listen to Dad's favourite one-liner: "With such scores, I'll not accept you even as a clerk in my own office!" And today, I can see his premonition tending to be true. The placements are approaching, and as of now, I don't have any reason to feel very safe and secure.'

'For once, can you stop correlating grades to the quality of job you are going to get on campus?' Sameer frowned, slapping Aryan lightly at the back of his head. 'There is a world of knowledge beyond these meaningless GPAs! That's what you need to really look at.'

'Yes, I know,' Aryan said, 'but would you mind explaining that to my folks too? I mean, really, half the tension and pressure is made up because you know the kind of expectations they have pinned on you. I wouldn't have been making a big deal out of this placement phobia had I not somehow associated it with the pride I intend to salvage in my parents' eyes. After all, I want to see that, some day. I want them to pat my back some day and tell me that I have done them proud. If I recall well, that has not happened to me ever. Landing a good job once, I feel, might give me the redemption I am looking for.'

I looked at Aryan. I wanted to return the same encouraging words that he always did when I was in the pits during exams, but I was at a loss for words, for my story was not much different. The only difference was that my parents had been much more liberal. Despite all my waywardness, they loved me and had always provided me that elasticity in time to grow up. Sadly, I too felt I had stretched the elasticity way too far. And it indeed was time to shape up. It was time for redemption.

'You are stretching it too far, Aryan,' Swapnil said, 'I don't know, but do you really think your parents aren't proud of you simply because you have not been outstanding in your academic endeavours? And even if you think that's true, you have time to redeem whatever you have to. And I can assure you, you are on the right track. I understand there is a tinge of anxiety, but trust me, we are all going through the same phase. But like everything else, this too, shall pass.'

'I hope so.' Aryan said absently, looking into his empty glass.

'For my sake,' I smiled a plastic smile, 'I want you to hope so. For it is hope that people like you and I live on!'

'Yes, and be thankful it's only your grades your parents bug you about,' Sameer said. 'My mother has been pestering me for the last one year, reminding me how old I am getting, and that I should respect the familial tradition and find a suitable match soon. I mean, how can you call me old? Look!' He pulled his face forward with his palm dramatically, rubbing his clean shaven face in a gesture of childlike innocence.

'You must be kidding!' Aryan said in surprise.

'I'm not!' Sameer said. 'The last time I went home, Mom thrust some pages up my face, some printouts of profiles of a couple of chicks, taken from some goddamn matrimonial column. No, wait, they weren't chicks. Their pictures looked like the "before" part of a fitness centre ad, but even that was beside the point. Man, you should have read their profiles. "Myself, a sweet, simple, homely girl who likes making friends and friendships. I adjust in all environments. I look for nice, sweet dream man who has similar interests!" Now if that does not really arouse any interest in my mind, I can't be blamed!'

I laughed out loud. 'Yeah, that must be a sore alright! But you might get luckier on your next visit home!'

'No way, are you nuts?' Sameer shot back. 'I am now so disillusioned I want to stay away from any such potential mess. I don't know if I must thank Soha for this, but my experience with her has taught me not to trust anyone. And I am afraid it is turning out like that; I find it difficult now to trust anyone - absolutely anyone. So then tell me, what's the use of getting somewhere, where there is nothing but pain and disgust?'

'Your problem is that you generalize about as quickly as you trust,' Swapnil said. 'Firstly, I think you were too quick in judging Soha to be the right person for you. Secondly, having done that, you have brought it out on yourself rather harshly. I'll tell you something. I have a girlfriend now for six years. And you know what? There is so much love in me that I know I can never let it out. And it's not been easy for me either. Nazneen is a Muslim, and her parents are dead opposed to this relationship. But it's faith that has kept us going. I have that faith in her which has convinced me she's never going to leave me. To reach that level of faith, you need time. I don't really think you gave yourself that time. But once you give that time, and realize you devoted that time to the right person, it can be the most beautiful thing that could ever happen to you!'

'How do you plan to take it forward from here?' Aryan asked. 'Because I am sure this relationship is going to draw a lot more flak in time to come.'

'Two things are very clear,' Swapnil replied, 'one, that we are not going to let go. And two, her parents and relatives are never going to agree to see us together. In that case, we'll be left with only one option: to take the path of rebellion.'

My eyes widened in astonishment. 'You mean you might run off with her?'

'There's every possibility!' Swapnil grinned. 'Sounds real filmy, doesn't it? Well, we have exploited all other possibilities but to no avail. I also offered to her parents that I was ready to convert to Islam if that made things better. But they were not impressed anyway.'

There was a brief moment of silence. We looked at Swapnil, and then at each other, too stunned to speak. Sameer got up and walked over to the DJ, asking him to change the jarring music to a softer genre. Aryan signaled the waiter for another bowl of nachos. And I, continued looking at Swapnil, with admiration and amazement. *Sounds filmy indeed,* I said to myself. But knowing Swapnil, it was not absolutely unbelievable either. Sincerity prevailed in whatever he always said or did, and if he said that there was so much love in him for Nazneen, I knew he really meant it. Converting his religion for that love, then, was a menial ask.

'C'mon, guys don't look so shocked!' Swapnil said, clapping his hands to recall everyone's attention. 'Knowing the place I hold in her heart, offering to convert my religion was the least I could do for her. And I don't think there's anything wrong in that, is there?'

'No, there's nothing wrong,' Aryan said, 'in fact, I am really in awe of you at this moment, man! Now this is what you call true love or what!'

'Whatever you choose to call it,' Swapnil shrugged, 'all I know is that it's a two-way process. I would not have probably thought of such a huge step in this direction had I not seen similar grit from Nazneen's side. Because at the end, all said and done, love too always comes with conditions attached. For me, those conditions mean that the other person loves me just as much as I love him or her. If that condition is met from the other side, then no condition is too big for me.'

'Precisely,' Sameer raised his thumb in a gesture of acknowledgment, 'and the reverse is true, too. Loving someone who does not love you as much in return is a wasted exercise, for the only outcome it yields is grief and disappointment. And sadly, the person who causes it doesn't even feel the minutest pinch of remorse. Especially if the person is someone like Soha, she exults at the fact that she has had the potential to shatter someone's emotions.'

'Every girl is not Soha,' Aryan said, 'and she's paying for whatever she did. The whole world knows what she is, and today she's blatantly ignored and sidelined by everyone in college. And strangely, I don't feel sorry for her.'

'Yeah, I agree, Soha was one bitch of her kind alright,' Sameer nodded his head. 'And I don't feel sorry for her either. But somewhere in my heart, I am grateful to her for having taught me a lesson that maudlin mentalities are going to get us nowhere. Your love's got to be too precious to be squandered over someone who does not appreciate its worth.'

He rested his head back against the sofa, closed his eyes and took a long puff of smoke. The anguish that hid behind his shut eyes was more than obvious to us. Much as he tried to bring himself across as a person who was indifferent to the indifference shown by people around him, there were times when he exposed his broken heart and injured ego. And that night, as the liquor flowed in endlessly, the dormant pain inside him spoke things that were never discussed before. And each word of his was a stark truth that peeped into my life as well - a truth that I was unwilling to accept. My affection for Naina had reached conspicuous levels of late, but what was more conspicuous was her increasing indifference and a distance she was almost consciously, calculatedly creating between me and her. I had begun to notice how I was steadily losing position in her list of priorities. While I could confidently claim that I was there to lend her an ear whenever she needed me to, the same was not quite the case with her. There were times when I wished to share with her some concerns that lurked in and pestered my mind, and all it would cost her was an hour off from her purportedly hectic schedules. But most often, my requests were turned down curtly, mostly without even bothering to find out the reason why I needed to talk. Each small instance of this kind began to aggregate into one big question: Was she incapable of appreciating the worth of my affection for her? If that were indeed the case, and if Sameer's statement was anything to go by, then my love and affection were not worth squandering over her. I confronted her on the matter a few times, but the only response I ever evoked from her was that we were two different persons, and it was not possible to perfectly understand each others' needs at all times. They were vague and fragile arguments, but they always won, backed by her reassurance that things between us had not and would not change. In each of our discussions, she implored me to believe that the notion I harboured was baseless, founded on my own set of parameters that she could not subscribe to, but which in no way lessened her affection for me. I, for my own sake, willed myself to believe her, thus blinding myself to the reality that was unfolding before me, slowly but surely.

'Nakul…' Sameer leaned forward and spoke, cutting through the silence.

'Yeah?'

'What I just said applies to friends too, nay?'

'What are you getting at?'

I knew what he was getting at. He was reading my mind, and I hated that.

'I'm talking about your growing fondness for Naina, and the lack thereof, from her side.'

'I have a set of people for whom I can go an extra mile,' I said, 'and you guys too are a part of that. Alright, I agree I might be going overboard at times, but then that's me.'

'Yeah, that's you alright,' Sameer said, 'but you'll feel the pinch when you find that others are not you. With hand on heart, tell me would you not expect Naina to be just as sensitive to your needs? You definitely would. And when the reality will deviate from your belief, even little things like not being asked to come along for a movie will hurt deeply. I mean, look, she's been a friend to me too, and I hate saying this about her. But knowing that even among all of us you are the closest to her, I thought I must warn you of what can follow.'

I shuffled around in my seat in embarrassment. Just like Sameer, I, too, often failed in hiding the affliction I faced due to the thousand implications I deduced from Naina's changing behaviour. And the placebo to my affliction was always my frail attempt at refuting my own implications.

'The movie thing did not affect me one bit,' I lied, 'I don't expect people to be answerable to me for everything they do.'

'That's nice,' Sameer smiled, 'if that is the truth - though I understood otherwise from your behaviour the next morning. If I were you, though, I wouldn't be affected by it. For knowing Naina as a friend, I wouldn't expect better than that. She's anyway hardly with us these days, thanks to her newfound friends and her so-called "pressure of academic performance"!'

Aryan sensed the discussion leading to an ugly scene as he saw my expressions turn livid. 'Take it easy, Sameer,' he said.

'You know you really need to shut up now, Sameer,' I shouted, 'I am not going to listen to another word against her. My opinions are not as juvenile as yours, so I don't need your smart sermon. Definitely not from someone like you, someone who can't handle his own…'

I bit my tongue as Swapnil kicked me in the shin from under the table. But the damage was already done. I had just reminded Sameer of his failed, pseudo relationship with Soha, and I found it to be one of the stupidest things I could have uttered. What followed was a painful minute of silence I wished would have never come. In a high-voltage emotional impulse, I had managed to hit Sameer where it would hurt him the most, and I could not stop cursing myself for that. We sat absolutely stunned, nobody knowing what to speak. I tried to continue eating my nachos, but couldn't stop my fingers from trembling. The clamor in the pub fell deaf on my ears, and I felt myself go numb.

'Thanks for reminding me, Nakul,' Sameer finally spoke. Tears filled his eyes, and shame and guilt filled mine. 'I'll keep that in mind. But if some day you do feel I made some sense, do come and tell me so.'

I didn't respond. We all went Dutch on the bill and made for the hostel.

CHAPTER 21

Worthless Dependence?

'Are the fourth trimester results going to be included in the CGPA to be presented at the time of placements?' I asked, stretching myself in bed on a Sunday morning.

'Yes,' Swapnil said, without looking up from his book, 'but why do you ask? You said your grades don't matter to you anymore!'

'They don't,' I said, 'but imagining that they would still make a difference to me might be my only motivation to study!'

I dug out four monster-sized books from the heap formed in my cupboard.

'What should I begin with?' I asked.

'Start with *Brand Building*,' Swapnil said, 'it's the easiest.'

I opened the *Brand Building* book and took a deep breath, resolving not to let the microscopic font of the mammoth 500 page material deter my intent. The inertia I felt before beginning to prepare for end terms was not a new phenomenon, only that this time I had decided not to let it prolong much, and had hence commenced my preparation a good one week before the exams. Notwithstanding the harsh reality that my grades were already screwed beyond repair, the least I could do was to salvage some pride and try and push my score to a presentable 3.0/4.0. I was admittedly better equipped this time. I had learnt a lot from my mistakes in the previous terms and had got a fair idea of how much of facts and how much of jazz our professors expected of us. *Whoever preached the advice to be precise and "to the point" in an exam must be dreaming,* I concluded. I prepared a list of all the Kapferer Models, the BCG Matrices, and the McKinsey 7S Frameworks of the world, and thought of umpteen ways in which I could fit each of them at least once in the paper, regardless of whether or not they would make sense to an average mind. *You want models and pictorial representations, you'll get them now.* I went full throttle on the syllabus this time, but somehow the incident at the pub the previous night kept haunting me continually like an apparition. I could not bring myself to terms with what I had done, and somewhere lurked a fear that I had scarred the relation that Sameer and I had shared thus far. And while I continued to maintain that he was no authority in telling me how to behave with a third person, I also did admit to myself that it was unbecoming on my part to blow my top and strike a sensitive chord by reminding him how inept he had been at handling his previous relations. The famous duel between the ego and the conscience lingered, and I just could not get myself to speak to him. Getting a turbulent mind to focus elsewhere was a wasted effort, I found, even as I tried switching between four subjects every few minutes in the hope that I would latch onto something. But nothing seemed to help.

'Any news from Sameer?' I finally asked.

'Nope,' Swapnil said, 'but Aryan and he were on the terrace last night, and Aryan said he was still a little down.'

'Do you think I should talk to him?'

'I don't think so; give it some time to heal on its own. Maybe you guys can sit and talk it out after the exams.'

I walked to the beach to get some reprieve. The sun had come right over my head, and a warm gush of wind blew into my face as I stood by the beachside at that odd hour of noon. The dry sand was hot enough to fry my bottoms, and droplets of sweat kept running down my forehead. But the calm setting seemed to be the perfect way to get me revitalized. I hence lay idly on the sand, ignoring the heat that permeated through my shirt and toasted my back. Not a soul was to be seen on either side of the stretch, except a bunch of kids playing cricket about some hundred yards away from me.

I closed my eyes, and soon fell into a small snooze which got disrupted by some commotion. I woke up and looked in the direction of the noise. I saw that the kids had discontinued their game, and two boys, who looked the oldest and the most authoritative of the lot, had formed a panel of sorts, and were engaged in highly animated conversation. Before them stood a little boy, of no more than ten years, with a bat in his hand. He was evidently the youngest of them all, and was not from the "group". Following a lengthy discussion, the group members said something to the younger kid and shoved him aside. The boy quietly left the scene without showing any resistance whatsoever.

Disturbed by the treatment he got, I walked to the boy to have a word with him. I expected him to sit sullen with dejection near the group, hoping that the group would recall him after some reconsideration. But quite contrarily, he moved a good distance away from where they were playing their game. He had a tennis ball in his hand, which he started tossing as high in the air as he could, and then ran ahead to catch it. Much of a boring routine that it could turn out to be, he seemed to be enjoying himself, and was totally lost in his own game when I finally approached him. I noticed his brand new *Britannia* labeled bat kept on the side; even the plastic coating had not been removed. A sticker on the bat said: "With love, Mom and Dad!"

A birthday gift for the kid can't go unutilized, I decided.

'Hi there,' I said, 'why are you playing alone?'

'They say I can't play well,' he said coolly, continuing to play catch by himself, 'so none of them want me on their team.' He tossed the ball high in the air one more time, and came underneath to catch it in safe hands. He then turned to look at me. His face had no expression of self-pity. He looked reasonably content doing his own thing in one corner.

'Would you like to play with me?' I offered. 'I can bowl pretty well.'

That was a lie. I couldn't bowl for nuts, and it had been almost a decade since I had last tried my hand at cricket. But I felt it would make him happy, and moreover a little bit of exercise would do my pudgy body no harm.

'Yeah, sure I'd love to play!' His eyes beamed with joy. He thrust the ball into my hand, walked twenty-two yards away from me, prepared dummy stumps and took position at his crease. 'Shoot!' He ordered.

We played continuously for more than an hour, with him batting for most of the time, much to my annoyance. But knowing that it made him happy was reason enough for me to keep going on. He drove my rather straightforward deliveries in all directions of the beach, and I was forced to run after the ball each time. At the end of the game, I was sweating like a monkey, and decided that I had burnt enough calories to spare me the guilt of all the junk I would eat in the following week.

'Second innings?' He asked after we had both batted.

I sank my knees into the soft sand. 'I'm done for the day, buddy! How about a snack now?'

We sat at a thatched stall to keep from the sun, and ordered two plates of *pav bhaji*. For the first time in more than an hour we actually got into a conversation, as we introduced ourselves.

'What do you do?' he asked.

'I'm doing my MBA,' I explained, 'it's a two year post graduate course…'

'Yeah, I know,' he said.

Smart kid! I didn't know at ten what an MBA meant. Even at twenty two, I didn't think I exactly knew what an MBA meant.

'That must involve a lot of studying?' he asked.

I choked. 'Yeah? Ahem…yes, it does…involve a lot of studying,' I said. 'It's a toughie. You plan to do it?' I punched him in jest.

'Of course not,' was his instant reaction. 'I'll do business.'

'What business?'

'Something in which there isn't much tension. Like owning a farmyard or an orchard in a foreign country. I've read it in the stories. Seems interesting.'

The kid's long term vision was praiseworthy yet amusing. I had a good mind to sound him that in no time social pressure would compel him to digress from his chosen path, and he would probably end up being some place else that he would learn to contend with. But I said nothing, as I didn't find it fair to shake a child from his dreams. I remembered how upset I had felt when my folks had laughed off my ambition as a kid to become a Bollywood superstar. In the current date, I was happy doing an MBA, because of the plethora of opportunities and the tempting moolah it offered. But my raw aspirations back then in my childhood had not factored in these important details.

'Where do you stay?' I asked.

'JVPD, Lane 6,' he replied. 'These guys playing out here are from my colony. I've played with them before.'

'I think you'd be better off playing with your group of friends rather than mingling with these big bullies, wouldn't you?'

'I don't stick to one group of friends,' he said.

'Why?' I asked, bewildered.

'I used to,' he explained, 'but often my friends used to go to the ground without informing me. By the time I would know they were playing, it used to be sunset. Dad then told me not to stick to just one set of friends. *It's worthless dependence,* he said; I'd rather look for new friends every day to fall back on, just in case I am alone one evening.'

'Your Dad's really wise,' I said, smiling.

As I took leave of the boy that afternoon, I felt grateful to him, for his story provided me the ammunition to analyze the argument Sameer and I had the other night at the pub. I only needed to drill into my conscience that it was easy to transpose the boy's larger-than-life theories into my own life. But then again, I was to find that larger-than-life theories fit

CHAPTER 22

The First Step To Success

Ruchi Karwal sat next to me, gazing me in the eye as she spoke something. But I was hardly listening, for I was spellbound by a charm that could potentially spark off a second Trojan war. Her sea-deep eyes and the poetic splendour of her appearance convinced me that she had it in her to stir the souls of the Keats and Wordsworths of the world, and force them to rewrite some of their classics in her name. I could have myself contemplated trying my hand at poetry right then, but the scene was far from being romantic. In her hand lay a fat textbook of Operations Research, and a small notepad. She pushed the notepad towards me and thrust a pen into my hand.

'I hope this is a good time?' She asked. Each time she blinked her long eyelashes, they closed and opened a world full of alluring mysteries.

'Yeah, why not?' *There can never be a good time for testing times like these, lady!*

I looked at the problem on hand, and cursed the instance of discussion in which I got carried away and proudly told her I was an "A" in Operations Research in the first year. As it were to turn out, she had to face problems in the elementary understanding of PERT and CPM, and now I was faced with the boring task of tutoring her on such a dry subject. More importantly, this task came at an inopportune moment, when I was myself burdened with no less than an upcoming term exam week, a burgeoning anxiety of placements, and three pending assignments to be submitted to Siren, who had threatened us with "undesirable consequences" on non-submission or delayed submission of the same. But chicks rule in the art of working their way out through that trademark innocent "oh-baby-will-you-help-me-out" expression, and this case was no exception.

'Chapter eight, page 134,' she said.

I flipped over the pages, straining the muscles of my fingers hard to keep them from trembling. As I opened page 134, I saw content that I thought I had mastered just over a year back. But that day when I revisited those forgotten pages, one year felt like a decade, and the entire script was alien to me once again. Through corners of the pages, hideous equations stuck out their faces and mocked at me. The numerical problems on CPM had strange, serpent-shaped diagrams that sent me reeling. I felt beads of sweat form on my temples even as I battled to save my reputation when it mattered the most. Ten minutes into re-reading the stuff, however, showed no symptoms that a former "A" in the subject should have shown.

'It'll take me a while before I get back into the groove!' I said sheepishly. Just then, my open laptop on the table flashed a message on the local chat messenger, which spared me the trouble of any further justifications I would have to give.

Aryan: Do you believe in the adage "Failure is the first step to success"?

Nakul: Yeah, I guess I do. Why?

Aryan: Good, then I have news for you. We have taken the first step. The results of the agri-business contest are out, and we are both out of the game!

I slammed the laptop screen shut, lest Dimple Doll should get to know of my meritorious feats.

'What's the matter?' she asked.

'Nothing much,' I said, 'I just got some urgent work. I'm sorry to be abrupt, but can we do this some other time?'

'No problem at all. But let's do it before my exams!'

'Sure.'

I found Aryan in the café, munching on a sandwich with some very leafy filling. He greeted me with a wide stupid grin as I walked in.

'Hi! Time to chalk out our next plan of action, is it?' he said.

'I can't see what's funny.'

'Don't get worked up,' he said, 'you didn't listen to the entire thing. We have two more contests lined up. One is some case study on some beauty product for women - it's called the Diva Touch, and the other is an ad-making contest. The first one is an individual thing, but the second is a team event. Do I get the honour of teaming up with such a gifted candidate as you?' He bowed his head in mock respect.

'I'm not interested,' I said dully, 'I'm now beginning to doubt whether I should have been here in the first place.'

'Hey, don't say that,' Aryan said, feeling suddenly miffed. 'If you are unfit to be here, then so am I, and so are lots others with us. Our problem is that we have undermined ourselves all the time. Trust me, we need to try again. We'll crack it now.'

'We are in want of time, my friend. Exams are round the corner too!'

'We'll create time, don't worry. And this time, there shall be no time tables, and no unreal targets. Let's just do our thing. It will work.'

'And no stupid theories of division of labour before exams, is that fine?'

'Perfect.' He raised his thumb up in the air.

'Ok, let's do it.'

'And don't ever again underestimate yourself. You are the undisputed king. Girls don't go to everyone to seek help in Operations Research!' he winked.

'You bloody rat! You've been spying on me!'

'Yeah, I have,' he grinned wickedly, 'now let's get down to work.'

He reminded me of the childhood stories we had heard, about King Bruce and the spider, and other fables that spoke of the miracles a strong will power could achieve. It was his energy that always permeated to me, and got me to run that extra mile during this crunch period. The night sessions in the library were now much more fun, though hectic all the same. We preferred the library to the hostel, because the sight of the bed in the hostel room served as a strong sedative, and we were not quite willing to dilute our resolve. Our discussions during the coffee breaks outside the college gate were now largely confined to the subject matter we were working on, and for the first time we both realized that studying was not all that difficult, and definitely not boring. It provided that feeling of satisfaction when I went to sleep each night that it was not just another day spent in the blockhole.

The examination week flew by as fast as it always did, only that this time we were not disconcerted with our performance. That our CGPA was anyway nothing to worry about anymore was beside the point. But we were reasonably satisfied with the effort we put in this time, making up for all the lack of interest in the management literature that we had shown in the first year.

We had discovered between ourselves a newfound quest for more and more knowledge by the day, although this was pretty late, judging by any standard. And admittedly, this turn over a new leaf was not a ramification of some inspirational flick of the likes of *Top Gun* or *Iqbal*, but was more in keeping with the Darwinian theory of the survival of the fittest.

The results of the exam came soon, and we were pleasantly surprised to find that we had actually touched the magical figure of 3.0, which would virtually be an entry ticket into the league of bright students, extraordinarily outstanding students and geniuses, in that order of ascent. But that didn't happen, as our aggregate still remained stuck below the 3.0 mark, getting us to carve out a separate category of self-defined geniuses anyway.

We sat on the hostel terrace that night. There was a nip in the air, and Miss Polka Shorts from the apartment opposite our hostel could be seen sitting by the window, chatting away on the phone like there was no tomorrow.

'Lucky girl,' I moaned, 'she has no worries. School life is so much fun! Go to school and attend a few classes. Enjoy. Recesses longer than the class duration. Enjoy. Come back, change and go play. Enjoy. Come back, have dinner and then watch TV. Enjoy. Finish your measly bit of homework and go to bed by ten. Enjoy...'

'Stop whining!' Aryan said. 'We can't crib, because we do half of these things even today. It's just that this career phobia has been getting the better of us. We need some respite, and we can't even afford it at this stage.'

CAREER: Something that I had been told and reminded about some hundred million times in all these years by parents, relatives and teachers alike. Something that I associated deeply with the expectations my folks had from me. Something that was going to define the rest of my life. From being a Bollywood superstar to a top cop to a cricketer to now being a high-flying corporate czar, my career aspirations had taken myriad forms in the last two decades. Looking from a broader perspective that night, I now saw my career path alright: a corporate executive in a suit-n-tie job, sitting in a swashbuckling chamber amidst a thousand pie charts and bar graphs waiting to be analyzed, and a chauffeur-driven snazzy car waiting to take me home after a grueling day at work. Beyond this, though, the littler yet critical details seemed blurred to my sight. I was still unsure of the sector I wanted to be in. I was still unsure of my dream company. There was also the lurking fear of the competition vis-à-vis the limited options that everyone was fighting for. And worst of all, as Aryan rightly put it, was the certainty in our minds that we were at the base of the lot. Less than two months hence, a moment was waiting to shape my destiny, and agreeably, it was largely in my hands to mould it the way I wanted to. And in such situations, undermining one's own potential was the most suicidal tendency imaginable. We reinforced into each other every other hour that we were going to "rock the placement scene" on campus, and that was the sole antidote to all our moments of anxiety.

'Have you thought of what companies you plan to apply to?' Aryan asked.

'You've asked me that question often before,' I said, 'and my answer hasn't changed yet. I have no prior work experience, *yaar*. I have no idea what sector or company would suit me best, so I might as well give everything a shot. But I'll primarily be focusing on banks and FMCG.'

'And what about IT? That's a sunrise sector too!'

'I don't know shit about IT! Are you going to go for it?'

'Nope, I don't know shit about IT either! We could have, though, had we not got addicted to that stupid Mario Brothers game we played on the laptop during our Information Systems lectures!'

We reminisced the classroom days of the first year, when we made it a point to reach class before 9 AM, just so we could book the last row for ourselves. Later, when reaching college early in the morning started looking like an ordeal, we began entering the classroom at night after dinner, and we would leave our notepads on the benches of the last row, booking our seats for the class next morning. Our ability to pull through the torture of nearly three-hour long classes corresponded directly to where we sat, and the last row was always a safe bet. One day, a classmate had brought to college the Mario installation CD, and we had found the urge to relive the days of childhood summers highly irresistible. That day onwards, Mario Brothers became a regular ritual in class for the last benchers.

Over time, in fact, I had come to closely relate my life in MBA to this game. As an explanation to the uninitiated, Mario Brothers is a game about a brave bloke called Mario, who is on a mission to get the princess trapped in a castle far away.

He encounters on the way menacing monsters and obstacles of various sizes - in particular the dirty dragon that spews fireballs at the final post just before Mario gets to meet his princess. Mario's job is to brave these hurdles in order to get to the princess. My princess here was that dream job that I needed - my singular motive of foraying into the game. The constant pressure of assignments and exams, the dejection that followed due to sub-expected performances, and a resulting lack of self-conviction had become the numerous monsters I had to fight. Fight I would, but the only difference between the two scenarios was that unlike Mario, I was not going to get three lives to meet the princess.

CHAPTER 23

Boys Don't Cry-I

'Hey, you there, on the last bench...'

There was no response.

'Hey there, sleepy head on the last bench, good morning!'

I woke up with a fright as Vandana elbowed me hard. 'Wake up,' she whispered, 'he heard you snore.'

Through red, puffy eyes, I saw the class burst into little giggles. Prof. Mahagaonkar stood in the centre of the room, staring at me with the bitterest smile possible.

'Could you please tell me what I just said?' he asked.

Obviously I did not know. And obviously he knew that I did not know. But his question made it certain that the class was in for another of his dissertations on the significance of discipline. I looked up at the board and saw some strange figures scribbled in his illegible handwriting, and tried desperately to get a hang of what was happening out there.

'I...er...' I mumbled.

'Singing lullabies are we?' he growled. 'You know what, when I was your age, we didn't have the facilities in our college that your institute boasts of. But we still made the maximum possible use of the sparse resources we had. When I began my first job, things were not easy. I often had to travel in the driver's engine room of slow trains in hot summers. And if today I am something, it is because of the self-discipline I practiced...'

'I'm sorry, Sir!' I tried cutting a long tale short; else he had geared himself up once again to embark on his usual trip down memory lane. And while his career's success story was an inspiration indeed, the marginal utility of this inspiration reduced each time he repeated the same story in class. Moreover, that day, my weary eyes had no capacity whatsoever to engage in a one-on-one serious conversation with him without those much needed forty winks.

I had stayed up through the entire night with Aryan, working on the preliminary round of the ad-making contest we had registered for. The requirement was to create advertisements for a newly launched matrimonial site, and we had gone bonkers trying to exploit all the latent creative talent we had within ourselves. We created a bunch of print ads, and a few funky video and audio ads as well, and were content with our effort by morning. But attending a 9 AM lecture after that was a tough ask, and staying awake therein was too high an expectation for me to fulfill.

In case of a freer say, I would be tempted to tell the professor that sleepiness was an inevitable part in everyone's biological cycle, and it was unfair for someone to tamper with it. But fortunately, common sense prevailed and I sat up straight, trying my level best to keep awake for the rest of the lecture. But the fatigue was getting the better of my intent, and looking at the projector screen was just worsening things. I couldn't talk either, as the eagle had his eyes now firmly set on me. In circumstances like these, written communication is the best camouflage, which gives you a means to divert your attention by talking to your neighbour, while giving the professor the feeling that you are one of those diligent geeks who makes a note of every word that he says in class. I pulled out my notepad and got into a written conversation with Vandana.

Me: Are you paying attention?

Vandana: I was, till sometime back. But I guess drowsiness is addictive. What's with you? Your eyes look like a pair of ripe cherries! You've been up all night again or what?

Me: Yeah. We were finishing the prelim submissions of the ad contest.

Vandana: Don't work so hard that you get driven to insanity one day! I think you are getting too worked up.

Me: Not at all! I have my career path clearly visible in front of me now, and I'll achieve it any which ways.

Vandana: And what is that, if I may ask?

Me: Earn big bucks for a couple of years in a big firm, and then use that money to open an orchard in some Swiss meadows. I'll earn good money lying in a hammock all day long!

Vandana: You have me jealous already!

Me: Don't worry, I'll invite you over one day. I'll also let you buy my fruits on discount! ... ...

The class ended sooner than I thought, thanks to the written dialogue we got into. I was almost about to tear the paper while I was about to leave, but changed my mind the next moment, folded it neatly, and slid it in the front pocket of my bag. It is said that it is small souvenirs like these that make up memoirs for life. I was not sure then how true the statement was. But I kept the token nonetheless, so when one day far down the line when I would come across it again, I could regale myself with the memories of these ephemeral moments which weren't there to stay too long.

'Oh, by the way,' Vandana called back as I was about to leave, 'Naina said she's planning lunch at Alfredo's with her friends, and she has asked us to join too.'

'I guess you guys go ahead,' I said, 'Aryan has a friend visiting him from Delhi, and Sameer and Swapnil keep too busy with their corporate project. So they won't come. I am also kind of beat, and moreover, I hardly know the Finnies. But I can go to a Barista with you if you have the time. It's been long since we've gone out.'

'Yeah, that's true, but this lunch has to happen today. I've already told Naina. Let's push Barista to some other time? Please come along for lunch today. You'll get to know the others only if you meet them.'

Convincing me to accompany them for a scrumptious lunch was never going to be difficult, and after little thought, I agreed to tag along. Moreover, I found it to be a good opportunity to undo some old knots formed between Naina and me. It had been anyway very long since we had gone out together, and as every day of our academic calendar progressed, the number of opportunities we had to be together kept getting reduced. Naina said once that our time here should have been remote-controlled, so we could pause and rewind instances at our convenience, and relive some of our most glorious times over and over again.

I couldn't agree with her more. But this day, this lunch in particular, was not to be penned down among the most glorious times spent over the two years. From the outset, it was not meant for me. Till the discussion at the table entailed things which lay in the realm of my knowledge, I tried mingling with the group. But in no time, the group dynamics took a sharp turn, leaving me lost and miffed. Whispers and intra-group jokes took centre stage, knocking me off the dais. I asked myself if that hurt. *Hurt, did you say? Imagine yourself amidst five people, two of whom you do not know at all, guffawing away like maniacs about something you can't get the hang of. And to top it all, they have the audacity to play Chinese Whispers on the table where you are dining, making sure all the while that you feel like a helpless zombie, staring at them dumbly and pasting an artificial smile on your face to ensure that you look social enough.* Yes, it hurt. More so, it angered me. Maybe I was too much of a perfectionist when it came to etiquettes, but here we just had basic courtesy taught in kindergarten that was lacking. What offended me even more was that Naina was the one who facilitated the plan, and although she was not directly indulging in the under toned tête-à-tête, she wasn't making any attempt to avoid it either. Friends are supposed to be able to tell at the drop of a hat that you are peeved at something. And here it was no big deal to discover that, as I was making a blatant display of my annoyance. Shockingly, she paid no heed to it, and completely ignored my presence at the table. Maybe my presence was out of context with the group's discussions. But then, it beat me why she even asked me to come along when all that was to be conveyed to me was that I was an external entity to the group. Maybe she didn't mean to do so, as she later claimed, but I didn't care. Vandana turned to me every now and then, picking an abrupt topic to talk to me, probably realizing that she had made a mistake by asking me to come along. But I was hardly in a mood to listen. I had a good mind to interrupt the discussion and recommend to them a good handbook on fundamental etiquettes that they so badly needed.

But I kept quiet instead, considering they were Naina's friends, and silently suffered through one of the most irksome hours I could remember.

I meddled with my phone for a while, trying to keep myself busy by playing around with its settings as we waited for lunch. To worsen matters, the service time at this restaurant was very high, which made the ordeal even tougher for me. Fortunately just then, I felt the vibrator of my phone drone with an urgent vigour. I sensed some respite from the tribulation and walked out to attend the call. I intended to make this conversation as long as possible so that I could avoid the others for a good deal of time. But when the going is tough, it's tough all the way, and even that wasn't to happen. I saw the phone that flashed on the screen "Aryan calling".

'Hello? Yeah, Aryan.'

'Dude, the results of Diva Touch are out,' he said. His tone was somber, something like I had never felt before. And I could feel it in my bones what he had to say. 'You haven't made it. They have selected twelve out of the applied fifty-five for the final round.'

'What about you?'

There was a split second of silence, and I knew that one of the two black sheep had just inched ahead.

'I'm through,' he said quietly. 'Hey but don't lose hope chum, you remember what I said, right? We are good, and we'll do well. It's just a matter of time.'

I felt my bones crunch, and my feet were shaky. I mustered the miniscule zeal left in my soul to encourage him. 'Hey, congrats! Of course we'll do it, man! For now you concentrate on the finals. Once this is done, we'll work on the ad-making finals if we get through the qualifiers.'

'You bet we will,' he said, 'we'll rock!'

Yeah, right! I stood outside for a couple of minutes, wondering what I was doing out there. One and a half years into the course, I had done nothing that I could be really proud of. It did not matter any more when the realization had dawned upon me and when I had gotten down to serious work. All that mattered was the gut-wrenching feeling of being an absolute moron who had come here for a two-year holiday, a moron whose under-performance had become as predictable on campus as the fact that pigs couldn't fly, a moron whose developed pessimism had left him with no clue to any direction that would show him some light.

I had heard that tears were a good medium to rid oneself of one's anguish. I tried exerting some force on my tear glands, but they played Brutus too. *I guess boys don't cry.* I got a hold on myself and walked back in. The jokes were still on, and I was still obviously not a part of them. But I did not want to be a part now either. My mind had transitioned to an altogether different plane now. I was eager to get done with the lunch as early as possible and head back to the hostel. It was time for some rumination again. But somehow, my hopeful eyes were still set on the friend who had always been my sink to unload the smallest of my anxieties. That day, however, I saw a very different Naina. I saw a Naina to whom my morose disposition mattered no more. Or worse yet, as she would often say in the future, the disposition was not evident to her. Given the average human propensity to be able to prioritize only certain things on top of the mind, though, I could not really blame her either. For a person who was in the midst of a thoroughly engaging repartee with a set of newfound friends, a dumb coot with a sulky expression could probably not have mattered less. The fact that I was always able to read her mind in her times of distress was beside the point. My mind was forced to flash back to the heated discussion Sameer and I had had at the pub the other night. But I convinced myself to dispel that thought as based on a one-off case assessment.

'What's up with you, Nakul?' Naina spoke to me for the first time. 'You look down.'

News flash: I am down. If anything, I did not want you to announce this in front of everyone. But alright, maybe we are getting somewhere.

'No, I'm not down. I am simply engrossed in trying to understand this seemingly interesting, animated conversation happening out here.'

I realized I had got a bit too conspicuous in my sarcasm, but I did not regret it. There was an awkward moment of silence when everyone looked at me, staggered. But the effect was short-lived. One of them leaned over Naina's shoulder once again and whispered something for the umpteenth time, and then let out a cheesy giggle. It was probably his opinion on me that he commented on, but I didn't bother to ask. I had quite a few comments in store for him too, but I resisted.

Thankfully, the lunch was not that time-consuming. The pasta and the burritos felt insipid to my taste buds. It was probably not the recipe, but a mix of the dejection due to the contest results and the severe irritation towards people around me that were to blame. While we waited for the bill to be brought on the table, Vandana quickly pulled out a tissue from the dispenser, wrote something on it, and passed it to me under the table. I unfolded it to read what she had written.

You really look upset. I didn't want to ask you in front of the others. But let me know if I can help. Coffee at 6?

I smiled. It did not take much human effort to lift someone from the pits. But there are few people who actually have the knack to do so, in fact, more so the will to do so, and Vandana was one of those very few. I looked at her and nodded. But the troubled mind still looked out for its guide, who was still far from getting even a whiff of what I was going through. While we were walking out of the restaurant, I pulled her back lightly and said: 'I feel like a short walk. Do you mind coming along?'

At two in the afternoon, it was no rocket science to figure that what I had proposed for was not a leisurely walk. It was a walk intended to let loose some agony. And if I were her, I would have picked the lead instantly.

'It's darn hot right now, are you kidding?' she said. 'Let's do one thing. We'll meet up in the evening. I'll call you around seven, is that fine?'

'Alright, thats fine.'

I trudged a long way back to the hostel. It was darn hot alright, but the temperature trouble was the least of the troubles.

CHAPTER 24

Boys Don't Cry-II

A dozen young executives in black business suits are seated in a large conference room in the head office, waiting for the chief to arrive. I walk in soon after, and occupy the chair at the centre.

'We are here today to discuss Bouquet,' I say, 'the new mid-segment women's perfume we intend to launch next month. We need to get on with the communication plan for the product across all major metros first. I need ideas from the team regarding the approach. What I suggest is we begin with a teaser campaign for the first fortnight...'

I hear a commotion among three executives at one corner of the table. They are almost in a huddle, and are hush-hushing amongst each other.

'Gentlemen, let yourselves be heard,' I say affirmatively, 'we are all a part of this.'

They don't pay heed to my warning. Instead, others on the table join the covert debate. I lose my patience after a few repeated warnings. Exasperated, I slam my fist hard on the table.

'You bloody louts! Where have you come from, some village or what? Do you realize there is such a thing as boardroom etiquette?'

'Pardon me Nakul,' one of them shoots back at me, 'but after due deliberation, we have realized we need to leave certain decisions to ourselves. So spare us the invectives. We shall be quite comfortable handling this case on our own.'

'I am your boss!' I shout back.

'We couldn't care less,' another replies, 'you have been no good of late. See what you did to Diva Touch! Thanks to you, it bombed in the market. I feel sorry to say this, but you are a failure…'

The alarm clock croaked aloud at 5:45 PM. I walked to the window of my room and pulled the curtain. The sun was about to set, and the otherwise beautiful view from my room looked very gloomy that day. It was a sickly feeling to be lying in bed in a semi-dark room in the evening, especially when almost every evening otherwise used to be so full of activity. My purpose of sleeping that afternoon was to catch up on the sleep I had missed the previous night. But the purpose had not been served, as I had simply lain in bed, turning around all the time, without managing to sleep for long. That is why I hated dreams. They were the biggest sign of insomnia. And things would be worse when the dreams would be unpleasant - dreams which connected me with my current reality. Again, my day till then had been largely disappointing with respect to everything one could possibly think of. To top it all, it was darn hot.

The *Business India* lay on Swapnil's bed next to mine, its pages fluttering under the fan. I lay sight on an article titled in bold: **American Management Association awards NRI**

Gerard Tellis the best management guru of the year. I browsed through the write-up and tried to imagine myself in that picture, receiving a medal from the prestigious institution, in keeping with my regular attempt to sustain the necessary "feel-good" factor within me. But my mind, which was clouded with too many worries at that moment, refused to indulge in any kind of vicarious thrill. I closed the magazine, changed quickly and set out to meet Vandana at Pop Tate's.

'First of all I am sorry,' Vandana said as we took our seats at a table. 'I realized you were really annoyed this afternoon with all of us.'

'Not with all of you,' I corrected her instantly, 'in fact only not with you. But the behaviour of the others was disgusting, to say the least. Was there a point they were trying to prove?'

I shouted out in a moment of rage, almost unsettling a grouchy woman sitting at the next table with her husband.

'I'm sorry, Aunty!' I mumbled a quick apology. Aunty was not impressed. She leaned forth and said something to her husband, looking at me simultaneously with a scorn. They may have thought me to be an insolent brute. But someone who knew the tumult I had gone through that day would have given me a second chance. Much to my discomfort, Aunty continued casting a sideward glance towards us for the rest of our discussion, with her ears cocked to pick any more juicy gossip possible.

'Did you discuss with Naina that you were upset about it?' Vandana asked me.

'Did she have the time to listen to me?' I asked. 'Couldn't you see what drama was going on out there?'

'I could,' she said, 'but I wonder if you noticed something else. Did you notice I felt just as uncomfortable there as you did? The only difference was that I did not make it evident.'

I was rather surprised. 'You were uncomfortable too? But you have gone out with them before too, haven't you?'

'Yes, I have. And I have experienced the same thing before.'

'And you still go out with them?' I asked, shocked. 'I mean I don't mean to stoke your thoughts on this, but if I were you...'

'Yes, but I have a different view on this,' she said. 'Naina is my best friend and she means a lot to me. I can't help but ignore certain small things like these.'

'I have been noticing that the distance between us has grown in the past couple of months. There used to be a time where she was the only one I looked to when I needed to talk about something. Now she doesn't seem to care.'

'That can't be true, Nakul. It's just a phase of tension right now for all of us before the placements. Give her some concession, she is just as busy these days as you might be!'

'I don't buy that. It doesn't take me too much to attend to a friend's despair however busy I maybe. Sometimes even lending a patient ear for five minutes can help. But our girl here doesn't even shell out a minute. And somehow I feel she gets damn busy only when I am around.'

'I know how you must feel,' Vandana said, 'but I just want to give you one piece of advice: Never try and expect someone to give back to you in the same measure as you give them, because mismatches in the equation will always exist. If you can't follow this policy, there will be no end to your despair.'

'And how easy is that?'

'It's not easy at all,' Vandana smiled, 'and that's why we all are in despair at some point of time or the other! It's just that we all know what the ideal solution to this despair is. Now the one who gets closest to implementing the solution in practice is relatively the happiest of the lot!'

'How good are you at implementing it?' I asked.

'I suck at it!'

It was a relief to hear that. The bitter experiences I gained not only taught me important lessons in life, but also became an incidental excuse for my alliance with Vandana to increase multifold. Thereon, we never missed out on opportunities to remind each other on various occasions that the mind must not expect from people what is not meant to be. We knew that we both sucked at implementing this in practice, but we were confident that one day we would together learn to conquer this weakness of the mind.

As we prepared to leave that evening, Vandana turned around and said: 'Remember one more thing, Nakul: the only way to resolve issues with anyone is to talk it out at the earliest!'

'Alright, Ma'am!' I smiled and left.

My watch showed 19:40 hours. It was a good forty minutes since Naina should have called me. After a few worthless battles with my ego, I took out my phone and called her.

'Where are you?' I asked.

'Hey, I am out with the Finnies shopping,' she said. 'I was getting bored sitting in the hostel throughout the afternoon, so I thought I might as well pass some time at the mall!'

Pass some time! So now if spending some time with me were to be the last of 'n' things to do on earth, she would create an (n+1)th thing and rather "pass some time".

I could feel my lack of desire to talk any more at that point, but I forced myself. 'I thought you were going to call me and meet me around seven?'

'O shit! I am so sorry; I completely forgot. I am really, really sorry!'

'You forgot?' I asked, shocked beyond belief.

'Yeah, you do know me, don't you? Silly me!'

'No, unfortunately I no longer believe I know you well enough.'

'Hey, don't say that! I said I am sorry. By the way what is it that you wanted to talk about? I did feel in the afternoon that you were distressed.'

'We'll talk about it if and when you have the time. Thanks for asking anyway.'

'So you are still angry, are you? Ok, how about breakfast tomorrow at 9? Crepe's Station, Carter Road. I'll call you in the morning. You can pick me up and then we'll leave.'

'Whatever,' I said dryly, 'whatever is convenient to you.'

The gate of the community park was surprisingly open till late that night. I walked in and sat down on the swing.

'What's up, buster?' I heard The Voice again.

'Don't you know what's up? I feel on Cloud 9!'

'Right, I know. Nothing's up actually. It's the pits for you. But ever wondered who has thrown you into the pits?'

'Who?'

'You, yourself, idiot! You rise from hibernation almost towards the end of the timeline, realize you have done nothing in life so far, and expect a miracle to happen suddenly! And when the miracle does not happen, you go around like a fool expecting others to provide you a healing touch!'

'And what is wrong with that, may I ask? When I have been with people in times of their need, why can't they? Or are you saying that I was more altruistic than I needed to? I am sorry; there was nothing I could do about it. That's me.'

'What you did was your wish,' said The Voice, 'now what others are doing is their wish. You don't and can't exercise control over others.'

'Then what do I do?'

'Sit and brood over the matter, and end up wasting more time, which you could otherwise wisely invest towards your primary objective of coming here for an MBA. I think you are such a fathead that even a thousand Sameers and Vandanas will not be able to drill sense into you. You are stuck in the swamp, and you have an option to work your way out on your own. But you are still waiting for a friend to give you a helping hand - a friend who, justifiably, will not prioritize your needs all the time. Think about it fast. Let not the swamp swallow you.'

'I know for a fact that I can't change myself. Maybe I am just too good for some people, but then things will stay the same. Does that mean I should allow for these differences, accept people as they are, and still call them my best friends?'

'Just like I told you before, at the end of the day, when you look around you, you are all alone.'

'That's not the answer to my question.' I said indignantly.

There was no response. 'Answer me,' I shouted. 'I need an answer to that one!'

I was pulled out of my delirium by the beeping tone of my cell phone.

Message from: Naina

Text: *Hey Nakul, the Finnies forced me to come along with them to the Hyatt for a midnight buffet. It looks like I'll be very late by the time I get back to the hostel. So the breakfast plan tomorrow may not be possible. I am really sorry for this. We'll talk later.*

Message sent at: 00.35 AM

The Voice was gone. But I did not need that answer from him anymore. Answers were beginning to unfold on their own.

CHAPTER 25

You Have Done Your Bit

January 2, 2006: 9 AM

"FYI- Meet regarding the guidelines and instructions for the placement week: New Auditorium, 3 PM"

The message lying in my inbox folder stared firmly into my face. I broke into a little sweat even as I felt a mix of anxiety and excitement churn within me. *Why MBA?* One question asked a thousand times by a thousand different people, a question asked a thousand times by us to ourselves and to each other, was now going to be answered in the coming week.

The auditorium was flocked by the entire batch at 3 PM, as we waited for Nilesh and Arvind, the chief placement coordinators from the junior batch, who were to detail us about the saga that was to follow in the coming week. The hum in the crowd reminded me of the first day in college, when we were addressed in the same auditorium about what expectations we could keep from this course in seeing us grow and evolve as individuals. Come January 2006, and I could clearly feel the evolution I had undergone over twenty months. Well, almost. From being a care-two-hoots brat unsure about his future, I was now a sincere, diligent workhorse unsure about his future. But I never stopped trying to find out where my future lay. Everyday a new ambition took birth, which fizzled out in a poof the next day by way of reasoning and debate with colleagues and other acquaintances. FMCG companies provided the much needed exposure in a career of Sales & Marketing, but the grind on the field there was grueling, and according to many, not suited for the kind of person I was. Banking jobs gave you good money, but the pressure of monthly number targets was a killer. IT jobs gave you that luxurious lifestyle that you could die for, but closed all doors for you to any other sector in the future. I had given up fighting these several contradictions and had left my mind open to all options. It was another matter as to how many options remained open to me.

The charm of a coveted MBA degree from a premier institution had appeared alluring from the outside. But once in there, it was a laborious struggle all the way. Sailing high on the utopian cloud of doing a course as prestigious as an MBA could be a perilous proposition, for it could potentially bring you down with a thud with one prick of reality. Unfortunately, I was a hapless victim of that prick. I sensed a tad late in time that I was just one of the hundred plus MBAs in my college and just a speck among the millions of MBAs across the globe, and a mere certificate in my hand was not going to take me to that zenith I had once aimed for.

Fortune, though, did finally begin to show some favour during the latter phases of my endeavour. Aryan and I were selected for the final round of the ad-making contest, and traveled to Indore for the finals. We also notched up the final victory in the contest, and the elation we felt at that moment was magical. But a one-off victory was not enough compensation for twenty months of hoboism. Instead, this victory served as a catalyst for us to press top gear in the nick of time, as we saw ourselves clinch quite a few titles in our kitty in the month before the placement week. There was now ample of stuff in hand to decorate my CV for the D-day. There was a heapful of confidence I had finally generated in myself. And the prize money I earned with each victory was an added bonus, used mostly to repay outstanding debts to friends.

The other aspect of my evolution as a person was my approach towards people around me. But sadly, I still resided in Utopia in that context. The Voice was right in saying that a thousand Sameers and a thousand Vandanas would fail to drill into my fat head that what I demanded of people, however close they were to me, was too much. All it essentially took was understanding the simple science of human psychology that no two humans thought alike, and that any given subject would be treated differently by both. But for a mind fettered by the fundamentals of a philosophy stating that close friends were the ultimate healer to all worries, taking this flight to reality was a humongous task.

Naina and I tried to bridge the gulf that had inadvertently developed between us. To be fair to her, she had also given the attempt a fairly good shot, or maybe the best in her capacity. Unfortunately, her best was just not good enough for me. She confronted me often, and tried explaining to me that things weren't as bad as I was making them out to be. And like every such discussion we had previously, we stayed at status quo.

'I truly value the association I've formed with you, and can't let such discrepancies affect it,' she had said. 'I promise you that I did not intend to be so insensitive towards you. It's just that I failed to realize then that I should have been with you...' *If you failed to realize that, what's the value of the association you claim to have formed with me?* '...Maybe that's my weakness, and I accept it. But I want you also to accept my callousness as a part of my nature, and not link it to how much I value our friendship…'

I desisted from arguing with her much further than that, but I harboured my reservations against the genuineness in her explanation. Callousness in one's nature is one of the easiest yet the flimsiest method to escape the simple truth that someone whom one may have considered to be a close friend at some point in time did not matter any more. This did not make that someone a bad person. Badness is anyway a relative term, and I was no authority in labeling anyone so. But it just goes to show how unimportant you can become to someone over a period of time. And when that same person says that he values your friendship, the paradox becomes impossible to digest.

'…My ways of expressing my affection and concern may be very different from yours,' she added. 'But that will not make me care less for you than what you care for me…'

My reverence for the relation I shared with her had reached an invincible status during the period of our summer internship, when she had been the guide I needed to get out of my project blues. In turn, I could not help but try and bury a thousand deeds of callousness that she showed any time in the future, and believe that she cared for me as much as I did for her. Or maybe again, the belief stemmed out of my need for her care rather than the reverence for the past association. Consequently, I kept hunting for her "different" ways of expressing her alliance. Till the last day, I could not find them. But over time, I had stopped complaining and had accepted this situation as it was. Or so I might want to say.

'Friends, we have two important announcements,' Nilesh cut in through the commotion, bringing me back to the scene in the auditorium. 'First, the CVs of students who applied to the following three companies - International Confectioneries & Foods, Royal Westend Bank, and Home Solution Paints - have been screened, and the list of students selected for the final round of the group discussion and interview has been put up on the notice board.'

I don't remember what the second announcement was. I don't think I had heard it either. It was probably something about the dress code and the customary instructions about the discipline that was expected to be followed while companies were on campus. But the weight of the first announcement was too heavy for anyone to care to lend an ear for the second. No sooner did the session end, than the batch made a dash for the notice board in unison. A large crowd had already surrounded the area by the time I reached there.

'Tell me, what's the scene,' I shouted out in a quivering voice to Swapnil, who was right in the front. 'And if it is a bad scene, don't shout it out loud.'

Swapnil scanned the computerized sheet over and over again, and then turned to me grimly.

'You aren't there,' he said.

'In which one?'

'All three.'

'Sorry, what did you say?'

'All three,' he repeated.

His words felt like a blade cut through my most sensitive veins. But then, *boys don't cry.* 'Aha,' I smiled, 'like I should be surprised!'

I wasn't surprised. I was, in fact, too dumbstruck to react. I slinked away from the crowd, trying to duck the inevitable question that was to be shot at me. Needless to say, I could not duck it for too long, and each time it was asked, it felt like a thousand needles wound my cachet. I was first stopped by *Khadi Kurta,* the top ranker of our batch, who, in the past too, had shown his extra eagerness in knowing how other people were faring as compared to him.

'Hey buddy!' *Khadi Kurta* said, 'What happened? Are you in?'

Buddy? In two years, Khadi Kurta never bothers to find out my first name, and now when I least need to address his questions, I become his "buddy".

'No, I am not. All the best to you, anyway.' I tried pacing my steps to get the hell out of there.

'You are not there? Not in any of them?' he shouted in a fit of astonishment, ensuring that half a dozen other "buddies" around would come and ask me the same question.

'No.' I said.

'How come?'

"How come"? There must be a thousand stupid questions that could be asked to someone, but this one simply took the cake. For one, it quashed the entire objective of pacifying the aggrieved, if that was the objective of asking the question in the first place. Secondly, it was a redundant question that the aggrieved would never be able to answer.

'Oh it's nothing,' I said, 'I just turned into an altruist and decided to make way for all you "buddies"!'

Khadi Kurta gave out a light guffaw and then, much to my relief, carried his pesky self to some other corner of the college.

I suppressed a glut of emotions within and scooted around the campus, looking for the farthest possible spot from any more such buddies.

'If I can suggest something at this stage,' Swapnil said when he found me in one of the remotest corners, 'it will be that now stop thinking about what is gone. Maybe those profiles weren't cut out for you. Just plan on whatever lies ahead now.'

'Yeah, you are right.'

'Nothing's lost,' he reminded me, 'there are hundreds of companies coming, and we still have a few days. We need to just apply ourselves into it now, and there's no reason why we shouldn't succeed.'

'Sure.'

I sat in the lawns, reviewing my CV before I could try my luck with the other companies. I plugged some music to my ears, but on this occasion even this most loyal ally could not mollify my misery. Braving a situation as grave as this seemed daunting enough. But equally challenging was the effort to mask the misery, so as to avoid sympathetic looks and unsolicited advices from everyone who came by. But my expressions were a giveaway to everyone. Everyone but Naina. Sitting less than twenty feet away from me, she feigned complete ignorance of my dismayed look, and sat discussing something with the Finnies. She did render a couple of quizzical glances, wondering why I was sitting like mayhem had struck me. But she did not find time to spend a minute to come and lend an ear. Fortunately or unfortunately for me, her indifference by then had brought me to a stage where I just couldn't care less. I had just been shown the door by the first three companies on campus, and there was anyway nothing she was going to be able to do about it. Moreover, had I confronted her on the issue of her insensitivity one more time, she would have come up with yet another super ingenious justification – that she understood me to be of the kinds who would prefer staying aloof in times of agony rather than allowing someone to scratch my wounds further. Any attempt to counter that justification would mean reentering that round of debate that did not have a solution. For want of time, mood and patience to do so, I decided against it and left the scene.

Just then, in what could be the worst timing possible, I got a call from home. And if masking my disappointment in front of colleagues was difficult, then camouflaging my shaky voice from my parents was next to impossible.

'How are things shaping up?' My father asked.

'Things are fine.'

'You don't sound like they are fine.'

'No, they really are,' I defended, 'it's just that I am caught up with some last leg preparations.'

'I hope you are not under any kind of tension due to the placements?'

'No, there's nothing like that.'

'Good, there shouldn't be. We just want you to remember that for us, all that matters is your happiness. You have done your bit, now leave the rest to destiny. Even in the worst of circumstances that might yield, we will be there to support you.'

'Thanks Dad,' I said, 'your support is all the motivation that I need.'

You have done your bit. I felt a lump in my throat on hearing those words. The realization that I was very likely to raze their tower-high expectations to rubble pained me immensely. It was a crying shame that I was on the verge of letting down the drain the best opportunity to express to them my gratitude for all those little things they always took care of to ensure my happiness. A brew of guilt, insecurity and helplessness gushed up my system, looking for a catharsis to explode. But I somehow managed to place the valve tight on.

'I'm leaving for the hostel,' I told Swapnil, 'there's no point sitting here. I'll see you later at the room.'

'Alright bro,' he said, 'and play it cool. Remember that you are not the only one going through all this. Everyone here has an anxiety of his own to handle. Those who handle it well come out the earliest.' I nodded in acknowledgement and walked away.

Just near the turn towards my hostel, I spotted something that would be rather unusual for a society as plush as Juhu Scheme. On a road that connected two rows of bungalows, belonging to arguably the most high-profile citizens of the suburbs, lay a huge, stinky heap of rot comprising stale vegetables, unfinished gravies thrown out of kitchen windows, rotten fruits and what have you. On any other day, my first reaction would have been to hurl a thousand curses on the irresponsibility of such citizens who otherwise boasted of being among the high-flier elite club of Mumbai, but lacked basic civic sense and concern for hygiene. That day, however, my attention was entirely gripped by something else. On top of that mound sat a wiry old man, who had both his arms cut off from the shoulder. His skin was wrinkled and scarred by wounds that looked decades old. The lines that contorted his senile face and those two eyes that had sunk in, shouted out loud the saga of his life. But they were still probably not enough to fathom the intensity of the afflictions fate had served upon him. Despite all this, he showed no signs of remorse or complaint. His face looked calm and content. I watched in horror as he bent down over the heap, and picked up with his mouth one among those dozen grotesque, decayed fruits. Something that yielded an intolerable stench till more than ten feet away was now being chewed happily by someone. The thought made me feel nauseous. He bent down one more time to gobble another smelly substance, but this time I did not allow him to.

'Wait,' I shouted out from the other end, and ambled across the road. I reached for a packet of biscuits lying in my bag, took it out and offered it to him. The man let out a feeble, almost sardonic smile, and I realized that he had no hands with which he could accept the packet. Embarrassed, I muttered an apology, and opened the packet and laid it on the ground, a little away from the heap. He now shifted position, arched his back one more time, and happily feasted on the biscuits. As I walked away, I observed a twinkle of gratitude in his eyes.

It's a pity that in this avarice for something that lies away from us, we often end up disregarding what we already have. We all come across incidents such as these, which remind us to thank our stars for things that we have that others may not. Life is unfair, but in a way it is so for everyone. And such incidents only reiterate a wise saying that however bad things may get in your life, remember that worse things can also happen. Sadly, again, we are never able to rationalize. We crib about the lack of facilities and infrastructure our cities have, but we forget that we inhabit a free society. We crib that we got into a certain "X" institute or course, instead of the "Y" that we aspired for, but we forget that we are lucky enough to get an education. We crib about one out of ten people who do not behave with us the way we want them to, but we forget that there are nine others who can give us a reason to smile. And despite such heart-rending incidents helping us take a peek into some elements of wisdom, we let these thoughts evaporate soon, and we start cribbing again. I was no exception, but thankfully this incident gave me at least a temporary spurt of a much needed vigour during what I would describe as one of the most defining phases of my life ahead.

While climbing up to the third floor of my hostel room that evening, I instinctively turned back and went down one floor below. I walked up to 204 and rapped on the door. Sameer was rather surprised to see me.

'Are you busy?' I asked after a brief moment of awkward silence. 'Or do you have a minute?'

'Come in,' he beckoned.

'It might sound funny, coming after such a long delay,' I began hesitantly as I sat down, 'but I wanted to apologize to you for what I said the other night.'

'Go ahead!' Sameer grinned.

'I apologize!'

'I'm glad we finally talked it out, pal,' Sameer said, 'I was afraid our egos were going to ruin our friendship. But I do wish this had happened a bit before. We ended up sulking for quite some precious time. In fact, even I should have apologized for what I said. I did go over the top that night!'

'No, you didn't,' I corrected him, 'in fact, I now do subscribe to everything you said that night.'

'What do you mean?'

'Just some bitter almonds I bit en route...'

'I got it, mate,' Sameer interrupted me, 'you need say no more. For now, forget everything else. We have something big at stake right now!'

I felt hugely relieved that night. I had re-injected some faith in myself and was prepared to face the battle in the coming week. I had almost fallen asleep when I received a message from Naina.

I know you were upset about the company results today. But don't worry, things will fall in place. I should have come and talked to you then, I know, but given the friction that we both have been feeling for some time...

The last few words of that SMS did not register with me. *Thanks for the pep talk,* I punched in an SMS in reply, and switched off my phone. I smiled to myself and went off to sleep.

CHAPTER 26

Judgement Day

January 11, 2006: 7.30 AM: Placement Week, Day 1

The peaceful bliss on Swapnil's face as he lay fast asleep that morning reminded me of my first afternoon nap of the school summer vacations, when I would come back after unloading the burden of the last exam of the year, and sleep like a log of wood. Understandably, the bliss on his face was much higher in magnitude, because he had just accomplished what he had set out to Mumbai for. The previous day, slated as Day Zero, saw some of the most coveted and highly rated organizations visit the campus one by one, picking roughly twenty. Although the official dates of the campus placement week were to begin from January 11, these were the companies, which, on account of the respect they commanded, always insisted on being the frontrunners in the herd. Swapnil and Sameer were among the first twenty-five to get placed on Day Zero, having clinched the prized Home Solution Paints and International Confectionaries & Foods, respectively. Day One was also host to some of the best companies, next only to the likes of those that came on Day Zero. The list of students screened for the Day One companies was to be put up in the lobby at 8 AM that morning. With an ounce of hope and a prayer in my mind, I had woken up early that morning, so that I could get there in time and check if I had run into any stroke of luck just yet.

I came out of a quick shower, squirted out half a tube of gel onto my hands, brushed it through my hair, and combed it neatly. I ironed my business suit and polished my shoes at least twice each. If sophistication indeed carried marks, this was something I was surely not going to let myself lose out on.

I was arranging my certificates and other interview-related documents when I noticed a folded piece of paper lying near my pillow. It read:

Hey Nakul! All the best for tomorrow. Do wake me up at 7:30 in the morning. I'll get ready and come along to college, just in case you might need any help out there.

He was still in deep slumber. *A slumber of well-deserved contentment,* I decided, *should not be disturbed.* But I made note of the gesture, one very typical of Swapnil - the kind of gesture that would leave an indelible impression on you, simply because the gesture, rare of its kind, was thoroughly genuine in its tone. Friendship was expressed, after all, more through gestures and little through words. Swapnil was one of those, very few perfect friends, who actually knew these little nuances of friendship. I envied him, and always told myself that if I could be someone else, I would want to be a Swapnil. A thorough gentleman with a divine heart, everyone knew it was impossible not to love him. And with each such selfless gesture, he reinforced that belief in us. I almost idolized him subconsciously in an attempt at getting close to being that perfect being that he was. I probably never could, but I thanked myself each day that I at least found a friend in him.

'Are you ready?' Aryan asked as he walked into the room, wearing an uncharacteristically tired and worried look.

'Yeah, almost done. Why do you look like you've seen a ghost?'

'Don't ask me stupid questions,' Aryan said, 'isn't it natural for me to look anxious today!'

'Why, you have always propounded the theory of self-faith,' I mocked, combing my hair once again. 'Now on the D-day, such a statement doesn't sound good coming from...ahem, "Your Highness"!'

'My theory was just that - a theory. Beyond those tall words I am also but human. Now will you hurry up? We are not going to attend a wedding. That's the fourth time I am watching you comb your hair. The panelists are not interested in seeing your hairdo. They'll be keener to know what lies beneath it!'

The college, though, did resemble in parts a marriage hall. The front gate had a carpet rolled out for the executives visiting for the recruitments. The lobby at the front section of the building had a line of students from the first year, waiting to welcome the guests, who were about to start pouring in, in big numbers.

'This extravagance is making me all the more nervous,' Aryan said as we entered the building. 'Why are they making it look like something so big?'

'Listen Aryan,' I pleaded, 'with great difficulty I have managed to gain some composure, and this has been largely with the help of your repeated reassurance that "we will rock". So now will you stop being a moron and shut up?'

'Go right in,' I heard a very familiar voice call out to us. I turned around to see Ruchi Karwal's beautiful eyes look at me, only this time from much closer quarters. The same mile-deep dimples that pierced her cheeks, and the same ivory skin, looked even more impressive that day. The poet in me was ready to surface again, but then again, the timing was unapt.

'Go right in,' she said, pointing towards the library. A tag she wore read "Placement coordinator". 'The schedule for the day must be put up there.'

'Ok, thanks,' I said. 'I didn't know you were coordinating.'

'I just pulled myself in yesterday,' she smiled, 'for want of anything more purposeful to do. If nothing else, I could act as a good morale booster for my seniors!'

'You bet you could,' I said, almost to myself.

'Huh?'

'Nothing, forget it,' I said. 'I got to move now, shall see you later.'

We entered the library, looked around the room, and saw around a hundred faces that looked like they had been watching one of the Frankenstein classics. The scene bore a strong resemblance to a butcher shop I had seen in Juhu Galli a few months back. The only difference was that the chicken in this room looked well-dressed, with nicely starched shirts, matching ties and business suits, waiting to be offered at the guillotine. We had been repeatedly issued memos instructing us to dress dapper for the placements, put a tiepin preferably, and, oh yes, also a handkerchief in our trouser pocket. It made me feel I was still a kindergarten kid who was likely to wipe his perennially running nose with his hand in public. I wondered if the college authorities thought being well-groomed would more than camouflage a suspected lack of intellectual prowess we were likely to display in the interview room.

'Get the resumes of the entire marketing batch down to the library…immediately!', Nilesh squealed into his walkie-talkie piece. 'Bytesphere should be on campus any moment now. We don't even have the resumes assorted yet!'

"Bytesphere should be on campus any moment now..". What? The words reverberated in my mind like a pair of tongs hammering away at a nail in the wall. Albeit a clichéd statement this, but time had really flown by. It seemed like yesterday when I first met Aryan, and discussed the companies we would fancy getting into, two years down the line. Two years! In case of leisure time at hand, I would have sat down to try and recall all the active, passive and hyperactive days that had shaped these two years. But at the moment my quivering limbs and the butterflies in my stomach forbade me from doing so. Bytesphere, one among the largest IT giants, was expected to recruit in large numbers, or so was the speculation doing the rounds. Being an engineer by qualifications, I did suit the requirements of the company, as its HR executive had mentioned beforehand that they would prefer looking at students with an engineering background. My anxiety was confined only to the first stage of getting my CV selected, post which I was pretty sure I would hit the home run. But that far, lady luck had been playing truant with me even before I could see the threshold of the first stage.

My alarmingly low grades had ensured that I could warm the bench for the initial few company processes that took place the previous day, and it seemed highly likely that there would be some more such companies in the morning shift on Day One. My confidence had stooped to the pits earlier when I was told that I was one of the only twelve unprivileged students out of seventy-eight who had not even made it through the round of resume-screening for Home Solution Paints. I forced myself, however, to keep up the courage, steel myself. "It's just a matter of a few more hours", I told myself. Or was it? I tried to keep my mind diverted by playing 'Mario Brothers' on my laptop.

Almost an hour later, there was an announcement of Flash Consumer Durables having reached campus for the process. The large projector screen in the library was finally switched on, even as the placement volunteers began to feed in the list of students screened for Flash.

'Are you game for Flash?' Aryan asked.

'Yeah,' I said, my eyes fixed on the projector screen as the cursor moved along at snail's pace. 'The more important question is if Flash is game for me.' We watched with bated breath as one more verdict began to appear before us. The cursor ticked one step forward as each letter of each name appeared on the screen.

'Why is the goddamn thing so slow?' Aryan said irritably.

'It's the machines,' I reasoned, 'they are overloaded and beat. Our college has been using these babies for the past two decades, I should guess.' Slowly the names came on display.

1. Abhinav Chopra
2. Rahul Mehta
3. Nandini Tagde
4. Salil Gaur....

The cursor ticked in absolute tandem with my frenzied heartbeat, and the anxiety was getting the better of us.

5. Swati Shah
6. Aryan Nair...

'Dude, finally!' Aryan sighed. 'There's something to look forward to.' I gave him a quick embrace and then turned back to look at the screen, which still had the cursor ticking, just as slowly. Only now my heart was racing much faster.

7. Vinay Menon

8. N…

In what looked like an infinitely long pause, the damned cursor stopped right there. The machine was jammed, and while it tried to reboot, the "N" flashing on the screen gave me an unexplainable jitter.

8. Niraj Kaul

There was no further movement. The cursor finally stopped, and for a moment, so did the ticking of my heart. I looked with a limp hope at the guy feeding in the data. *Is the bloody machine jammed again?* Sadly, it wasn't. I saw to my dismay the guy get up from his seat and reach for the mike. 'These listed students are requested to move to room 38. There will be a group discussion for them starting in half an hour, followed by a personal interview.'

Aryan looked at me with an expression I would never fail to understand. As always, he meant to say something that would charge me, but stopped short this time.

'Don't worry about me,' I smiled, reading his mind perfectly. 'I have the hooks fastened; I'll get the fish soon! You go right ahead and crack it!'

'Thanks pal,' Aryan said, 'I'll keep you posted.'

Time dragged over that session, as a company or two would come in every hour or so to pick a few more students. Most of them were investment banks and credit analysis firms which were of no relevance to me. But the realization that my colleagues were getting on the other side of the shore one by one was unnerving. Just a while later, the projector also flashed a message saying that Vandana had got picked by Royal Westend Bank. It was a strange predicament for me. Glad that I was on seeing three of my closest chums placed, I found myself at a loss of energy and will to partake in their ecstasy. I felt like I was being pulled into a black hole for eternity, and as each second passed, the ray of light seemed more distant.

My patience began to give way. I went to the reception desk. 'What's the scene with Bytesphere?' I asked.

'It's expected around 10:30 AM. The list of selected students for Bytesphere will be put up on the second floor.'

My watch showed 10:20 AM. Three hours of unyielding patience and a pounding heart had been painful enough, but I was beginning to crack now. Forty-four students had already been placed, three of them being among my closest friends. I had tossed and turned in bed the whole of the previous night without blinking an eye, and had begun to feel the effect now. I put my head down on the table, and shut my bloody red eyes tight. Within minutes, I was woken by an excited voice. 'Nakul, quick!' Sameer shrieked almost into my ear. 'You've been short listed for the first round of Bytesphere! Move to room 21 for the group discussion immediately.'

'Sameer? What do you think you are doing here?' I asked, rubbing my eyes. 'You should be out partying, dude!'

'Go partying without you guys?' Sameer said, in a loud tone of disbelief. 'Man, do you really think that's possible? I'd rather wait here, so that at the end of the day all four of us can go party big time!'

'Yeah,' I said, 'it's been long.'

'Anyway now you'd better get going,' Sameer said, 'the group discussion is starting in ten minutes.'

The second floor contained the ruckus of a flea market. The already narrow lobby was swarmed not only by students waiting for their turn to participate in the group discussion, but also by students who were already placed and were there to boost the morale of their colleagues. Then again, there were students from the junior batch-those who were coordinating the various processes, and also those who weren't coordinating, but were observing the drama that they would be going through a year hence. I felt claustrophobic. I weaseled my way to room 21 to find out the group allocated to me.

'You are in Group 2, speaker number 7,' Nilesh said, 'and Group 1 is already in. So you go in next.'

I went slightly weak in my knees. Although I knew this situation had to come, it suddenly felt all so unexpected. I felt an urgent need to relieve myself, and headed for the restroom.

'What process?' asked a colleague standing in there, biting his fingernails.

'Bytesphere,' I said, 'I am going in for the group discussion next. What about you?'

'Same here,' he said, 'group 4. I am shit scared.'

'You bet,' I shook my head, 'this is the fourth time I am peeing in the last hour. I am damn nervous.'

A slightly elderly gentleman standing near the wash basin turned to me and gave a wry smile. I gave him a vexed look. It wasn't fair. *If only you'd put yourself in our shoes, Sir, you'd know that this was hardly funny.*

'You'd better get running, then,' my colleague warned. 'Group 2 must be about to start.'

I was back just in good time. 'Hurry up,' Nilesh beckoned as I ran towards room 21. 'Get in fast.' He thrust a piece of paper and a pen in my hand and sent me in.

Either the air-conditioner of the room had been kept on full blower, or I was still suffering from the edginess syndrome. As I faced the panel, though, I masked it with an affected air of confidence, and ambled to my seat.

'Please introduce yourselves to us,' said one from the panel, 'before we begin.'

As the introductions began, I perused the eleven students I was sitting with. There was a pugnacious look in every set of eyes, reflecting a warrior that had woken up after a long lull, now to fight the most important battle of his life. There were some faces among the eleven I knew more closely than the others, of colleagues with whom I had shared that occasional repartee in the classroom, and of a colleague who had confided in me one night about certain dark patches of his past. The tense ambience in the room, that day, misted up all memories with past acquaintances. What each of the twelve warriors saw in that room that day was the sight of eleven contestants fighting for one common prize. And each one believed that he best deserved the prize, and the weaker ones had to be vanquished.

'Your topic is "Technology in 2020-Where is India headed?"', announced one of the panelists. 'We'll give you two minutes to pen down your thoughts, and then you can begin the discussion.'

Like an unexpected lightning charging my senses, my mind instantly opened up to all that it could gather in one hundred and twenty seconds. I guess adversity always does manage to bring out the best of you which may have stayed undiscovered until then. In less than thirty seconds, I had gained enough ammunition to rant over the next twenty minutes. I sat looking at my watch, waiting for the two minutes to end, so that I could begin.

'Technology, as we see today, has shown unprecedented leaps globally,...' a girl from the group suddenly spoke aloud. I was startled. I looked at my watch. There was still a minute to go. *Whatever happened to the mentioned two minutes?* Before I could react, there was a barrage of arguments being shot at from all directions, and in no time, the room had turned into a full-fledged war zone. Temperatures soared and voices roared as each person tried to make himself heard in the melee.

'India is definitely seeing technology flourishing by leaps and bounds...' said someone.

'But we also need to consider the cons of any kind of progress...' the first speaker butted in again, on an entirely different plane.

'Please let me finish...'

'...Weapons of mass destruction are just one of them...'

'Let's all have a chance to speak...' someone else complained.

'...so it will be important for India to channelise its resources towards a humanitarian purpose...' the girl went on nonchalantly.

'I completely agree with you, but...'...

Agreeably, the atmosphere in the room hardly resembled the decorum that would be expected in a formal group discussion. But with a mere twenty minutes playing a vital role in determining what lay ahead, decorum had to be the last thing on everyone's mind. After waiting long enough in vain for the noise to mellow down, I ruptured the flow of the debate with my own set of points I had jotted down. Under a single breath, I spewed out as much matter as I could. The holler continued from all corners, but I raised my voice loud enough to ensure that at least the panelists, if not the others, heard what I was saying. Then arose another round of debate over what I said, and the skirmish erupted again.

'That's it, my friends,' a panelist banged his palm on the table after twenty minutes. 'That was very interesting. You may leave for now.'

I sensed a tinge of sarcasm in his remark. But the ruckus during the discussion notwithstanding, I was reasonably satisfied with my bit.

'How did it go?' asked an eager Sameer, outside the room.

'It was just about OK,' I said, actually unsure about my prospects on that front. 'There was a mad crowd in there.'

'There's good news, guys!' Vandana came running through the crowd, waving her hand frantically. 'Aryan is in for the final interview with Flash!'

The good news beside, the information boded well for me too, for Aryan was one person whose luck had almost always run parallel to mine, whether on a crest or on a trough. There was now reason for me to believe that something nice was going to happen to me soon. Though a frivolous premise, the correlation gave me comfort during that long one hour before the list of students selected for Bytesphere's final interview would be announced.

'That's great,' Sameer said, 'and congrats to you too! You got a prize catch!'

'Thanks,' Vandana smiled gleefully, 'it's a big relief!'

'You had to get it, girl,' I said, 'you are a rock star! You deserved it!'

She gave me a hug. 'You deserve it too, Nakul, and you are going to get it soon!'

It was definitely not *soon* by any measure. The next hour felt like eons of wait, till the announcement of the final five interviewees was finally made.

1. Paurush Vaidya
2. Niharika Sinha
3. Nakul Kapoor...

I jumped out of my skin. I didn't care to hear the last two names. 'Was that my name he called out?' I asked.

'Yes, indeed it was,' Sameer slapped me on the back, 'this is it, Nakul!'

This is it! 'I suddenly feel I am not prepared for the interview!' I panicked.

'Relax,' Sameer said, 'we all feel that way. When you go in there, just be yourself, and it will all be fine!'

'And just in case you need some last minute *gyan*, I have it right here for you!' Swapnil shouted, brandishing a piece of A-4 sized paper from a distance.

'What's that?'

'It's an article I dug up just for you,' Swapnil said, 'it talks of the new process modeling techniques IT giants like Bytesphere have come out with. But if you think you don't want to get worked up at the eleventh hour...'

'Are you nuts!' I said, snatching the paper from his hand. 'Knowledge never harms, at whatever hour. Albeit late, I have realized this today!'

I tried wolfing down as much information as I could in the thirty odd minutes I had, before the coordinator called out my name.

'Nakul, come on,' he said, 'you are in next.'

'Rock dude,' Sameer and Swapnil called out from behind, 'go gas!'

The interview room looked eerie. There was a deathly silence about the whole place that shot a chill down my entire body. But I got even more petrified on facing the panelists. On a panel of three members, there sat in the centre the same gentleman with the wry smile in the restroom. *You've had it, Nakul, you've so had it!*

'Are you feeling better now, young man?' The gentleman in the centre smiled. He was flanked on his sides by two HR executives. On the left was a young man, presumably a young entrant, who probably had got his first chance to give back to me what he might have received a year back from someone else. On the right was a slightly older, plump lady, who sat reclined in her chair. For most of the time she did not speak, but just shot a continuous mean glance at me. If her objective was to unsettle me, I was just making her task very easy.

'I am quite fine, Sir,' I said, donning the most suave, confident smile I could. 'Thank you!'

Thankfully, there was no further discussion on the restroom episode. They began the routine round of questions about my family, hobbies, strengths and weaknesses, all of which I answered with reasonable ease-thanks to the hundred sessions of mock interviews I had practiced with Aryan on the hostel terrace on many a night. *So far so good,* I thought, pretty smug with myself. But then came the first bomber.

'Tell us something about your summer project,' said the young HR guy.

No! There is no way I am going to share with you the laurels I gained there!

'Or no, wait,' he stopped me.

Thank you!

'Tell me about this robot project of yours,' he said, pointing at my CV. 'It interests me.'

What the hell is that thing doing here? I stared horrified at the line on my CV mentioning that I was a member of some geeky group that had built a robotic vehicle back in engineering days. I recalled then that on some godforsaken day, I had penned that feat down on my CV, and later, in the tense weeks that followed, I had forgotten to review my work on that project.

Well, then, here goes nothing, Nakul. "Go gas"!

I cautiously began, making sure I didn't fall prey to any trap by saying something I could not defend. 'It was a wireless surveillance system we had built, which contained advanced maneuvering capabilities and a micro-robotic gripper for handling small objects and remote vision…'

'Hold it,' said the man in the centre. 'We are not robotic experts, please! Explain it in a layman's language.'

Now, isn't this what I was really hoping to hear! I stepped up the "Go gas" spirit and shot off explaining whatever little I remembered of three years ago, in the most flamboyant style imaginable. I pleasantly surprised myself at the ease with which I went on, hardly bothering to recall the actual mumbo-jumbo that had comprised the building of the robot.

'So was it finally accepted by industry standards?' he asked at the end.

This was a tough one. For one, we had not bothered to find out whether it matched industry standards. And while it was perfect by our standards, I feared he would delve deeper into it if I told him so.

'No, there were minor flaws in it,' I forced myself to say. 'The IR vision capability of the robot did not permit it to see beyond a small range of distance.'

They looked at each other quizzically, and then the younger guy got a small nod from the man in the centre. They then quizzed me on a myriad of other topics, ranging from my marketing subjects to work ethics, a phase that I was well-equipped to handle without any major hiccups.

'Just one last question,' said the man in the centre, 'you seem to know a lot about everything that we discussed. The inter-college contests you have won also show exactly that. Then why are your grades so low?'

This was the biggest bomber, and that too just when I thought I had sailed to safety.

'They are low, I agree,' I said, maintaining the confident tone, 'but they are not reflective of my capability.'

'They are not?' he asked, astonished. 'I always thought they were meant to reflect exactly that!'

'I believe written exams actually cripple our ability to showcase our talent,' I said. 'In an exam with a stipulated time of two hours, we are expected to show on paper all the knowledge that we can, and that is not really an accurate measure of our knowledge. When we talk to people at leisure, like we have done in the last forty-five minutes or so in this room, we get a much fairer idea…'

I bit my tongue as I saw one of them break into a small giggle. 'That's a nice answer,' he said, 'you may leave now. But please stand right outside for a minute before we take a decision.'

I walked out with a dilemma in my mind. They were going to give spot offers to selected candidates immediately after the interview, and by the rules of the placement office in college, that meant I would have to take a spot decision to accept or reject the offer right there. The temptation to explore other avenues was great, but the insecurity about what possibilities lay ahead was even more severe. Moreover, Bytesphere figuring among the top companies that day, I thought it wise to grab the deal if offered. But the ominous sign was that the two candidates interviewed before me hadn't got the offer, and that meant a very poor conversion rate.

Naina met me right outside the room.

'What happened?' she asked loudly, in an excited tone.

'Ssh,' I cautioned, 'they are in there, taking a decision. They'll tell me in a minute. How's it been with you?'

'I am placed!' she nudged me excitedly. 'TFC consulting it is!'

'See, I told you!' I said, giving her a hug. 'You always had it in you to get there!'

'Thanks Nakul,' she said, 'and you know what? Your encouraging words time and again made all the difference. Especially that evening at the beach...'

'I'm not quite sure about that, Naina,' I cut in, 'I am really not quite sure how strong my presence has ever been for you. But I am happy for you anyway.'

Another potential argument on an oft argued topic was deferred, as the plump female executive came out. She looked at me and smiled, and then stretched her hand forward. *Does this mean "Congratulations" or "Thanks for coming, better luck elsewhere?"* I did not stretch my hand forward until she spoke.

'Congrats,' she chuckled, 'we want you to be a part of us. Are you willing to take the offer now?'

'Gladly!' I said, shaking hands with her. My hands trembled as I reveled in delirium and followed her inside to meet the other two panelists. When I walked out, I was greeted by a loud, congratulatory roar from four excited friends.

'Please people,' one of the coordinators pleaded, 'please maintain silence, other processes are still on here.'

But the celebrations could not wait any more. We began to walk down the stairway when we heard a commotion on the lower floor. We ran down to find Aryan being picked by half a dozen guys, being offered the conventional congratulatory "kicks and bumps", a typical symbol of celebration on campus.

'So we rock dude!' I said cheerfully, once the ritual was done.

'Yeah we do,' Aryan smiled, groaning with pain at the same time. 'I got Flash! And we reached the finish line together!'

The six of us got into a huddle, and once again broke into a raucous roar. After very long, we had found an excuse to celebrate together again. And this was the perfect excuse.

CHAPTER 27

Comfortably Numb?

Down to the last twenty-eight days of our most magnificent sojourn of two years, the atmosphere on campus began to strongly reek of farewell, and that left a queasy feeling inside me. The ecstasy of having achieved, by and large, what we had come there for, was annulled by the realization that we were to bid adieu to the joyride very soon. The lows of the joyride were surely not so memorable, but each low left me with a lesson to learn for the future, and I could only be grateful to the people and the circumstances that rendered those lows to me. The highs, of course, comprised the crux of the joyride. They were the strongest factors that helped me combat the lows. They also, of course, were the main reason that I felt queasy about the whole farewell feel around me. Twenty-eight days later, the path I would take would digress from that of the people with whom I had been through those highs and lows. And before I took the digression, I wanted to spend some time with these people, thanking them for the good times, forgiving or apologizing for the bad, and trying to undo some old knots. I only did not have that much time. Nor was there much to complain about, for even with double the available time that I had now, the feeling would end up being the same in the last twenty-eight days.

'I knew this time had to come,' Vandana said, her face drooping low, 'but now that it has, I don't feel like facing it yet!'

'Yeah,' I nodded my head approvingly, 'Naina's remote controlled time idea sounded very convenient to me. There would be just so many phases I'd like to rewind and relive. Likewise, there would be just so many I'd have wanted to hop skip and jump!'

'Or rather, maybe,' Vandana corrected me, 'you'd want to amend those phases instead of jumping over them?'

'I didn't get you.'

'You did get me, Nakul,' she said, frowning. 'I know you are not dumb. I've been watching what's going on. When was the last time you spoke to Naina?'

It was a long time indeed. And while this was far from the outcome I had hoped for, I had reconciled to the situation. Naina's ostensible unconcern had hardened me also to believe that this was the way it was meant to be, and I was now almost ready to let the parting note also contain the message that I couldn't care less than what she did. Only that would mean my injured ego trying to kill the conspicuous truth lying somewhere within me - that her self-professed callousness towards our friendship was a rapier that had left me with a permanent wound. And I would surely be kidding myself if I said that time would nurse the wound. All the time we had to nurse whatever wounds there were, was those twenty eight days. Talking things out was the only way to nurse them, but then again, each session of talking had always led to a non-sequitur dead end.

'It doesn't matter when I last spoke to her,' I said agitatedly. 'She must not have cared to notice that either. Now I'd just be doing well by not troubling myself with this any longer. I've had enough.'

'Suit yourself then,' she said. 'But just make sure you don't leave a task unfinished which might force you to say some time down the line "I wish I had..."'.

I did not want to say "I wish I had..." in the future. This was the only time I had to patch up whatever loose ends possible. And if I were to find one strong reason to do that, it was that I was the affected one in the whole story. It may not have affected Naina even minutely, but I was not going to let go without letting her know my opinion on the entire matter. I took out a sheet of paper, and let out a magma that had been concealed too long.

Dear Naina,

I don't even know why I am taking the pain to write this to you, because I have been seeing how inconsequential this discussion always turns out to be. The way things have been developing, I doubt whether you'd even care to read this. But still if it doesn't hurt much, extract five minutes from your precious time to hear me out.

You surely don't need to know what you have meant to me. Be it the times when you were a source of support and encouragement through my lows, or when I spent with you some awesome moments during the highs, my admiration for you and for the relation that we share had reached a level that I cannot articulate.

But somewhere down the track, things did go wrong. It's pointless trying to pass the blame or cite instances, but the underlying fact is that gradually and inadvertently, I felt a distance develop between us, which got worse by the day. I still can't figure out the reason; did I err somewhere on the way, or was it just a bunch of expectations I did not deserve to keep? Whatever it was, it's too late now to analyze and amend.

But before we part ways, I want to make clear a thing or two. Don't mistake my attachment to you as my weakness. In better times, your friendship was my strength. But today, the lack of it does not make me weak by any measure. I always thought our need for each other's friendship was mutual. But now when I see that you need me no more, let me tell you that I don't need you either. I jolly well understand that an excessive dependence on someone can jeopardize my sense of self-reliability, and I am not ready to do that. But at the same time I must inform you that the justifications you have always given me in terms of we being different people never went down as a good excuse for your indifference. It's very easy to get the monkey off your back by saying that you are a different person and hence find it difficult to live up to the expectations of your friend. If you think that's a great excuse, then I have a piece of my mind to share with you. However different two close friends may be, they are, more often than not, able to gauge each other's feelings right. In that view, then, your unresponsiveness to my need most of the times only suggests that the closeness I once thought existed was just a figment of my imagination, a mirage which I desperately tried to convert into a reality. But alas! I was wrong.

There were times in the recent past when I desperately needed to talk to you, when I was low, when things just didn't seem right, and where I felt that I needed the same Naina who had once been the sole friend I believed I could rely on whenever needed. I don't know if you've ever experienced this treatment, but suddenly when such a person turns his back on you, the soreness is very severe. I can hardly blame you for this, because come to think of it: you are not answerable to me for anything you do. You have a life of your own, and I can't expect you to change just for my sake. But the least you could have done is to have been honest; if not with me, then at least with yourself. Instead, you kept reiterating that you valued our friendship. And each time you did that, it reinforced a hope in my mind that there was scope for things to get better. You'd rather have told me upfront that I was a bug you could no longer bear. It would have made things much simpler for both of us.

Please don't even bother to reply to this letter, especially if you are going to repeat the clichéd argument that your ways of showing your concern are very different, and that I have not been able to understand them. Even if that is true, I am sorry to say that I don't subscribe to your explanations. If you think I am a kid whom you can convince into believing otherwise by way of such feeble arguments, you are sadly mistaken. I am a simple person who interprets things as he sees them, and then forms an opinion based on them, which can't be changed by merely mincing words. So you can tell me a million times that you hold our friendship in high esteem, and I will disregard your words as many times, simply because it does not reflect in your actions any more.

If you wonder why I never said this to you earlier, it is just because somewhere down in my heart, I still hold a lot of respect for you as someone who had once been one of my closest friends. And I know for a fact that this respect can never die.

So smile, Naina, for you have nothing to lose even after all that has transpired. For even if you disregard this letter as just another piece of paper and move on, you can rest assured that I will never fail you as a friend, in case you should ever need me again. Much as I might try, my reverence for you can never fade away.

I would only be extremely delighted if I were to believe that there could be a solution to this deadlock that we reached. But I know this deadlock is here to stay, and I am ready to reconcile to this situation. All that I can do at this stage is to assure you that I will always be there for you, no matter what. And I ask for no reciprocation in return any more.

Love,

Nakul

I grappled for over an hour to find the choicest words to send across my message with the strongest possible force. The funny part in writing the entire letter was that I myself felt I was making an extra big deal of the whole issue. If a patron of rational thinking read the letter, he might have dismissed me as insane, and I would also have no way to defend myself. For with all the respect and concern I could offer to my own emotions, I could not have, till the end, precisely pointed significant instances of Naina provoking me enough to get me to lash out so severely at her. Alright, there were times when I was deeply hurt, there were times when I felt she was thankless for all that I may have ever done for her. But throughout this phase, I constantly ignored the simple truth that you alone have the power to hurt yourself. You alone have the power to seal yourself against any potential heartbreak. I ignored the simple truth that what I saw her do to me was only a mild glimpse of how insignificant and inconsequential one's feelings could be to the world.

By the end of having written the letter, I was myself confused as to what the message was. Inwardly, I was battling a bunch of contradictions: did I actually want to tell her that I did not care about her coldness, or was I trying to plead her to try and be a little more considerate? Did I mean to be rude or contemptuous about her behaviour over the last few months, or did I mean to thank her for what a wonderful friend she had been earlier? My thoughts that showed on paper were no clearer than the chaos that existed in my mind.

I looked around for Naina, but I couldn't find her. I had developed a headache, and I felt the urge for buttermilk to soothe my nerves. Being a Sunday, the kiosk outside was relatively less crowded. I ordered buttermilk, and leaned against a car parked under the shade of a tree on the sideway. On the other side of the car, I heard two familiar voices engaged in a conversation of high emotional gradient.

'It's unfair to be judgemental about someone's loyalty as a friend,' I heard Naina complain, 'and Nakul has done just that. And that is what has hurt me so much.'

My ears pricked up. This sure made for some interesting hearing.

'He is not being judgemental, honey,' Vandana said, 'he has a point, the way I look at it. I don't say that you are at fault. But there can be a way to bridge these misunderstandings, can't there?'

'Misunderstandings can be bridged if both sides make an attempt, Vandana,' she said, 'I have tried explaining to him often that I care just as much as he does, but I am different, and so is my way of displaying that. But he is just not ready to accept that. It pains me terribly. I know he has always taken the utmost care on all occasions to see that he is there for me when I need him, and the truth is that even I am ready to do that...'

'I know that, Naina,' she said, 'but he doesn't. And this has simply strained matters between you.'

'Why should it have?' Naina shouted. 'I can't find a way out of this mess. I know for a fact that I can't change as a person. I can't suddenly become Nakul, and go that extra mile to ensure that I am the most perfect friend there ever was. I know I have my limitations and my weaknesses, which understandably, he doesn't like. But then if you have declared someone to be your friend, you should be ready to accept him the way he is, and not start drawing inferences from every action of his. The definition of someone being your good friend is when you don't start grading his allegiance with every passing day!'

She was one hundred per cent right in everything that she said that day. And I finally believed her in full earnest. I had been unreasonable, rash and biased in my judgement. My obstinacy had now led me to a stage where I could not convince myself that I was to blame too, for the chasm that had formed. Also, I could not, somehow, confront her again, and tell her that my faith in her remained unscarred. There were a hundred things I wanted to say, and a hundred that I wanted to hear. But there remained a lack of time, and a lack of opportunity. For all the time that remained, there was only so much opportunity as to regret over the potentially good time we could have had, which we lost out on, for reasons as frivolous as they could get.

'I understand,' Vandana said, 'but now just try and talk to him once more.'

'No, I can't! There is no way I am going to do that. With just four weeks left here, I don't want to leave on a bitter note. And talking to him on this matter has always yielded a very caustic end. I'll let it pass.'

'You mean you are ready to lose a friend?'

'No, I can't dream of doing that,' she said, 'but I hope that time will be the best healer. When I meet him sometime in the future, things will hopefully be pleasant again.'

I couldn't help but smile on hearing that. *Meet in the future? If wishes were horses…*

I took out the letter from my pocket, and tore it to shreds.

In an ode to the sweet sands of time,

I hear a promise made by a friend of mine:

Vast as may be the distances to gain,

She will turn back time to come meet me again.

Whiffs of this gale will revisit my memory,

But will carry with them a scathing accessory.

Yet when I take a fond trip down memory lane,

I'll want to trace back my steps and come meet you again…

I walked back towards the college gate. As I wound through the corner of the road, I saw a group of students from the junior batch sitting at the tea stall, sipping on *cutting chai.* I saw them talk the talk I once talked with my friends. I heard them laugh the laughter I once laughed with my friends. And realizing that I was standing at the exit way of that happy journey, I felt jealous. I tried to feel indifferent, I tried to feel happy. I looked around for The Voice, hoping to know, how, after all, could I try and feel *Comfortably Numb.*

CHAPTER 28

Out of Network Coverage

My room was in shambles. Two jumbo suitcases, smeared with cobwebs and dust layers gathered over two years, stood in one corner, waiting to be cleaned and repacked. A horde of books, loose papers, graded and rejected assignments, sat scattered on my bed as I tried to decide what went into the suitcase and what went into the bin. A half-open cupboard showed a glimpse of a stack of clothes lying in a mess. I had initially intended to begin packing all pieces two weeks beforehand so as to avoid getting worked up on the last day. But somehow the last day seemingly came sooner than I had anticipated. Or maybe it was sooner than I had hoped, for reasons more than one.

As I emptied the contents of my satchel, out fell a crumpled, half-yellow piece of paper, which contained a written chat Vandana and I had had in the class one day. Within minutes, I was reminded of countless such moments I spent with my friends, which I would just want to relive over and over again. And the reminiscence of each such moment only increased my resistance to packing off from there.

I glanced at the clock that ominously ticked away, closing in on the final moment. The letter of invitation for the convocation ceremony lying on my table read: Kindly ensure you arrive at the hall at 3:00 PM sharp. The proceedings will begin at 3:30 PM.

I had less than half an hour. I heaved all my stuff and dumped it into the suitcases, and made a dash for the venue. I was not really very late. As always, the time intimated to us was with a buffer, so as to ensure we would reach at the required time of 3:30 PM, and no later than that. But apparently, two years had been long enough for most students to understand this ploy of the authorities even as I saw lots of them trailing along slowly even after 3:30.

'It doesn't matter, you know,' Swapnil smiled when someone remarked he was one of the last to drag his lethargic self to the venue, 'they anyway couldn't have begun the show unless all of us reached. So why hurry?'

The heat of this April afternoon was merciless to say the least. Add to that a thick black convocation cloak wrapped around you, and a heavy black cap would make you feel like a microwave oven. But then, these accessories had their special significance. They were supposed to make you feel proud. So was I, but that feeling of pride was accompanied by a strange uneasiness at the thought that in a few hours, there would be some such people I would probably not meet again - some people with whom I would have hoped to stick on longer. But now that it were to happen, I wanted to get over and done with it as soon as possible.

But the wait seemed long while we waited outside the hall in two long rows, waiting for the chief guest and other dignitaries to arrive. A band of musicians in white uniforms, loaded with trumpets and huge drums, led from the front.

'I don't remember being made to feel this important before,' Aryan said, 'sure feels good!'

'There's more to come in the future,' Sameer nudged him, 'very soon you'll be in that.'

He pointed at a silver Mercedes that pulled in through the front gate. Two of the organizers ran to the car as it stopped, and opened the door for the chief guest, a president of one of the leading Indian banks. The dean and the university chancellor followed suit, and ushered the chief guest in.

After a long wait under the ruthless sun, the march finally began. The musicians began a clamorous symphony with the drums and the trumpets, leading the procession into the hall from the main entrance. Behind them trailed two long rows of hundred students each, barely able to contain their excitement in anticipation of the moment they had all looked forward to. As the procession entered the auditorium and up the aisle, groups of students from the junior batch stood on the side, cheering for their seniors. As I approached the central walkway to take my seat, Ruchi Karwal stepped up in the front, quickly thrust a note into my hand, and then went back into the crowd.

09833*#*976- Keep in touch, and all the best J

I turned around to look for her, but she was many rows behind. Moreover just then, the lights went off and the chief guest took the dais to begin his keynote address.

'My dear friends, I know you are all going to be eager to get to the final stage of this ceremony,' he began, 'so I am going to keep this very short. But nonetheless, there are a few things which, I feel, I would do well by sharing with you budding managers…'

His speech clocked a mammoth ninety minutes, and after every ten minutes, he gave a reassurance that he was going to keep it "real short". For a man of his stature, it was only natural to have so many things to advise on for our future. But the focus of every student was on that moment of elation, when the chancellor declared the convocation ceremony closed. In the true spirit of triumph and ecstasy, two hundred delighted souls sprang to their feet, and tossed their caps in the air as a mark of celebration. The batch broke into a deafening roar, followed by a round of congratulatory as well as farewell embraces to each other.

'Nakul, I am leaving,' Vandana came up to me and said, 'I have my flight at six. I need to leave right away.'

'Huh?' I was shocked. 'Are you not waiting until dinner?'

'No, I have my ticket booked on this flight. I need to leave for the airport from here.'

'I thought we would have time for a last chat…'

'There's never a last chat, Nakul,' she laughed, 'even if I were to leave tomorrow, we would have hoped for a last chat!'

I nodded. There were things that began to brew in my mind, an amalgamation of thoughts that I had in mind I would mention when we spoke for the last time. But in that moment, I forgot all that I wanted to say, and simply ended up muttering, 'I'll miss you!'

'Ditto!' She said as she gave a quick hug, and then walked away from me.

'Do we have time for a last drink?' Sameer came up to me and asked. 'What time's your train?'

'Eight-thirty,' I said.

'Cool, then,' Sameer said, 'come with us to the hostel, pack your bags and then we'll go to Enigma. You can leave directly for the station from there.' He paused, and then added: 'Unless you want to spend some more time here with the others?'

I saw Naina climb down the walkway, coming towards my side. Embarrassed, awkward, and at a loss of words, I slinked away into the crowd, tugging Sameer along. 'No, let's go!' I whispered.

The turnout at the pub was rather thin. Only two tables other than ours were occupied, and the room bore a dullness matched only by the insipidness maintained at our table. We sat through most of the hour in absolute silence, letting the drinks flow, and quietly watching the clock tick away rapidly.

'I think you must leave now.' Swapnil's sharp words finally cut through the stillness.

'Must I?' I asked, looking at my watch. 'Oh yes, I actually must! It's almost seven thirty.'

As a cab pulled over near the entrance of the pub, I turned to them and said, 'Adieus Amigos! Need I say that it was a pleasure knowing you guys?'

Aryan did not respond. He began meddling with his phone.

'Don't say adieus,' Sameer said, 'say something better.'

'See you soon, amigos?' I asked.

'That's better!'

I plunked my bags and myself into the cab, and sped off for the station, leaving behind three men who not only turned out to be my best friends, but also three different sources of inspiration for me; three friends who, in each of their unique ways, had shown me a different, yet impressionable view of life. I felt indebted to the allegiance we pledged, and in reciprocation, "see you soon" was the least I could say instead of an adieu.

I did not look back again.

The cab desperately tried to weasel its way through the nasty suburban evening traffic. But after a long battle with the numerous logjams, the driver dutifully ensured that I made it just in time. I hopped out with my bags and sprinted across to the fifth platform. The train had hooted its first warning whistle when I got on. I had barely found my seat and had begun to arrange my heavy luggage down under the seat, when my phone set off its noisy ring tone.

"Naina calling"-the screen displayed.

'Hello?'

'Hi Nakul,' she said slowly, 'have you left?'

'Yeah, I just sat in the train.'

'I thought you would have at least met me once before leaving.' I sensed a tone of agitation in her voice.

'I wanted to,' I said, 'but I was rushed up.'

The train now slowly began to chug away from the platform.

'I always knew you to be a guy who was never too rushed up to have a word with a friend.'

'Time and circumstances changed me, Naina!' I said sourly.

'Nakul, I know this is too late to talk about it,' she said, 'but I wanted to talk to you…about…things that have…gone haywire…'

As the train made its way out of city limits and into the rural outskirts, the mobile network began to go weaker.

'I know,' I said. 'I have myself to blame for it.'

'Me too,' she replied, 'but I still maintain...some of the....beautiful days...'

'Hello?' I shouted into the phone. 'I'm losing you, Naina. The signal's getting weak. I just wanted to say sorry.'

She tried squealing from the other end. '...sorry too... I didn't want... things...end...this way...'

'Hello?' I shouted again.

'I hope...keep in touch...?'

'Hello?'

I looked irately at the screen of my phone. The display bars of the network strength dipped low steadily. The bars finally dipped to level zero, and a message flashed on the screen, saying: **Out of network coverage.**

I felt like some fresh air. I walked out of the cabin and stood by the door of the train. Mixed with the deafening sound of the wind, I faintly heard The Voice call back to me once again. 'Like I said, at the end of the day, when you look around you, you are all alone...'

Index